WOMEN TEACHING BOYS
caring and working in the primary school

Martin Ashley and John Lee

Trentham Books

Stoke on Trent, UK and Sterling, USA

WOMEN TEACHING BOYS
caring and working in the primary school

Contents

Trentham Books Limited

Westview House	22883 Quicksilver Drive
734 London Road	Sterling
Oakhill	VA 20166-2012
Stoke on Trent	USA
Staffordshire	
England ST4 5NP	

First published 2003

British Library Cataloguing-in-Publication Data
A catalogue record for this book is available from the British Library

ISBN 1 85856 278 3

Designed and typeset by Trentham Print Design Ltd., Chester and printed in Great Britain by Cromwell Press Ltd., Wiltshire.

Introduction

The pages of the *Times Educational Supplement* in January 1998 were the scene of a debate or perhaps a spat about the question of boys and girls in contemporary schools. The exchange was between a distinguished journalist, Peter Wilby (1998) and two highly respected academics and researchers Caroline Gipps and Patricia Murphy. Both Gipps and Murphy (1998) have spent their careers researching into questions of equality and social justice and Peter Wilby has a strong track record over the same issues. What then could they possibly have found to fall out about? In fact the debate encapsulates many of the concerns that we have tried to address in this book. At least we answer one complaint that Wilby makes about Gipps and Murphy. Writing of their book *Equity in the Classroom: Towards Effective Pedagogy for Girls and Boys* (1998) he says

'All but one of the 18 contributions are from women – imagine the outcry if it had been the other way round.' Well, in this case the book has been principally authored by two men.

It may seem odd but actually we agree with Wilby and Gipps and Murphy. In the first instance Wilby makes the point that in the 1970s attention focused on the achievement of girls. Now that they are ahead of the game there is a refocus on boys. We argue in this book that this has the features of a 'moral panic' as originally described by Cohen (1987). As he says, tongue in cheek, this may result in the return to traditional roles. We wonder even whether the current concern for boys may be a backlash against the gains that feminists made during the second half of the twentieth century.

Gipps and Murphy's response is interesting in a number of ways and also reflects some of our concerns. They say, *'The underachievement and teaching of boys is generating rather more hot air than good strategy at the moment'* and we entirely agree. We will argue that both the causes of boys' apparent lack of attention to schoolwork and the solutions offered to it have a tendency to be unsophisticated and simplistic. We also say that in the case of the views of primary school boys evidence is lacking. Wilby accuses Gipps and Murphy of ignoring the question of a pedagogy for boys and instead producing a pedagogy for girls. We do not want to join the argument over this, but we do try to ask the question as to whether boys learn differently and should be treated differently from girls. Our evidence, as any reader who gets beyond this point will see, indicates that football is not the solution. Unsurprisingly, not all boys like football. As an aside we find it odd that the current Arsenal football team is being used to promote reading to boys. Wouldn't they be better promoting the learning of another language?

Wilby makes reference to how changes in society make male/ female role models more complex and difficult. We have some sympathy with this and examine the currently proposed panacea of strong male role models and mentors in schools. Our evidence suggests that much of what is being said is at best unhelpful, something we believe Wilby also feels.

Gipps and Murphy are concerned about the behaviour of boys towards girls.

> The real worry is not that the boys will smash the place up, as Peter Wilby argues, but that they are already smashing the girls up: there is increasing evidence of boys' growing misogyny, represented by bullying, harassment and name-calling, reported in schools from Africa, America, the UK and Australia.

We don't deny the existence of bullying or of boys' disruptive behaviour but, unlike these authors, we have attempted to get evidence about how boys feel. We find that often the fact that boys can be sensitive is ignored. So a major part of the book addresses itself to the question of how boys feel and whether they can express those feelings. We find that boys can and do want to talk about sensitive issues, but that the very 'crisis' of which they are part is denying them that opportunity.

CHAPTER ONE

How policy makers have created a 'problem-with-boys'

What policy makers believe and do

The furore over the behaviour and achievement of boys in primary schools is an old one. For instance Humphries (1981) records high levels of rebellious behaviour and dissatisfaction in the early years of the twentieth century amongst boys and girls. Earlier it was the 'bad' behaviour of boys that was often commented on by HMI. At this point in the 21st century we have returned to a major concern for the achievement and behaviour of boys. A wide range of commentators, politicians, policy makers, some educationists, academics and the media present a dire picture of the educational performance of boys. We argue in this book that this picture and the solutions suggested for it are misguided. The crisis is a kind of moral panic (Cohen, 1987) created by assertion rather than by the careful marshalling of evidence. The easy solution to the 'problem' of failing boys is to see them as requiring very different handling than girls. This includes assertions about the nature of boys and what they are interested in. What is being argued is that the lack of male primary school teachers is having a detrimental effect on boys and the easy solution is more men and 'manly things' in primary schools. A politician's view on this is well represented in the Education Secretary's speech of 20th August 2000.

> The myth among boys that it is cool to fail at school must be stamped out, Education and Employment Secretary David

Blunkett said today as he outlined a package of measures to narrow the gender gap in educational achievement.

Tackling this laddish culture will be at the heart of the new strategy. The Government wants to identify the barriers to boys' learning, including peer group pressure, and ensure that there are more good male role models to challenge boys' resistance to learning. The DfES will ask all Local Education Authorities to provide a detailed evaluation of the progress of local programmes to tackle boys' underachievement. Mr Blunkett put an obligation on all education authorities in 1998 to include such schemes in their Education Development Plans.

Mr Blunkett said: 'The gap that has opened up between the sexes at school is a long-standing and international problem for which there is no quick fix, but I am determined that our boys should not miss out. Let's not forget that the achievement of both boys and girls is rising throughout schooling. However, we face a genuine problem of underachievement among boys, particularly those from working class families. This underachievement is linked to a laddish culture which in many areas has grown out of deprivation, and a lack of both self-confidence and opportunity. (DfES Press Release 2000)

This is a bold statement of what the Secretary of State and presumably the DfES see as the problem, and a bold solution in the way it charges LEAs with the responsibilities for development planning and evaluation. In the light of this, it would be as well to ask whether there is an important difference in the scores achieved by boys and girls. Although it is an established fact that the effects of social class and ethnicity are critical to pupil performance in the construction of the gender gap these factors are totally ignored, except when demonising working class boys. The 'gap' is one of the two principle pieces of evidence used to support the argument that something must be done about boys and that that something must be unique to boys. It would then be as well to ask the question whether there is an important difference in the scores achieved by boys and girls.

Stephen Gorrard has been a rigorous critic of the use of statistics in education policy making (Gorrard, 2000). He is highly critical of the way in which the gap has been constructed. Although he focuses on Wales what he has to say about the methods of measurement hold true for England as well. He points to a lack of understanding of statistics and arithmetic amongst politicians and others as leading to the construction of problems where no such problems exist. Gorrard describes how 'the crisis narrative (of gender achievement) is at least over-stated and possibly incorrect.' One significant reason for this is the way in which numeric data are analysed and described. He identifies a confusion between percentages and percentage points and a lack of proportionate analysis as highly problematic. Secondly in the case of boys and girls, Gorrard argues the lack of comparators, in the case of boys' and girls' achievement the absence of historic benchmarks. In addition to this we would argue that the changes in the nature of SATs over time should make all commentators sceptical of their value as accurate measures on which to base policies and actions. Gorrard's third point is highly significant for this book. He notes that

> ... genuine proportionate analysis involves the use of contextual factors. Typically this involves trying to make 'fair' comparisons of the examination performances of differing groups of students, what has been described as value added. Despite the apparently wide acceptance of this principle (although analysts may debate the specific methods used), many of the proponents of the crisis account of British education still make comparisons on the basis of raw scores.

It is this 'fact', the gap in achievement, that leads to the current gender crisis and, as W.I. Thomas says, 'if men define situations as real they are real in their consequences'. Regardless of Gorrard's powerful argument or more kindly because they, politicians, policy makers etc, are in ignorance of it the boy problem exists. This book does not address the statistical problem but deals directly with what has been proposed by those who have both engendered and accepted the crisis.

W.I. Thomas's view that regardless of the 'facts' of the matter belief is more important is born out by the way in which central government has continued to stress the need for special measures for boys. The most important plank of this policy is the determination to increase the number of male primary school teachers for the benefit of boys. The question of the need for specific role models goes beyond simply finding men to teach boys. In a rather interesting perhaps extraordinary manner MP Dianne Abbott claims that for African-Caribbean boys white middle class women teachers might well be the problem. Originally stated on 8/1/02 in a fairly blunt manner

> .... a Labour MP (Dianne Abbott) claimed that black boys were under-achieving because primary schools were dominated by women teachers.

...the comment was later moderated/corrected in *The Guardian* report by Rebecca Smithers (2002)

> Diane Abbott, MP for Hackney North and Stoke Newington, said black boys needed boundaries and strong direction from 'male mentors' at an early age.

> She said primary schools had become a feminine domain and called on the Education Secretary, Estelle Morris, to recruit more teachers from the Caribbean.

> 'Certainly work that I've seen in the United States shows that where you can have more male teachers, particularly at primary school level, and male mentors, that does help some of these boys, both black and white, to engage in education,' she told BBC Radio 4's Today programme.

Dianne Abbott made what is probably the most strident comment on boys and achievement and specifically black boys and achievement. In January 2002 *The Guardian* reported a suggested solution to the boy problem.

> School standards minister Stephen Timms sought to defuse a row about the educational achievements of ethnic minority boys by saying young black men were being attracted into jobs as learning mentors who provide back-up to teaching staff in socially-challenged areas. But he admitted that the matter was 'a complex issue' and more male role models were needed in schools. (Smithers *op cit*)

What policy makers are basing their judgement on is common sense rather than evidence and science. This common sense view is reflected in a recent *Times Educational Supplement* article (Duffy, 2002) wherein it is confidently stated what the nature of boys is 'action-orientated – impatient, imaginative, willing to take risks' and that since 'boys' first teachers are women it's not surprising that some boys pick up messages that learning is really for girls'.

We have the context in which policy and practice in primary schools operates. Put simply it is:

- Boys have severe educational problems

- In primary schools they are taught by women

- To solve their problems boys need role models like themselves

- To some degree women teachers are both the problem and the cause of the problem

- Recruit more men into primary schools.

Self-esteem and role models
All of this is predicated on a view of the need for role models, made explicit by specific reference to male role models and if not teachers then learning mentors. It is appropriate then to try to unpack the theories that might underpin this requirement for models. Crucial to the policies sketched out above is the idea of self-esteem and in particular high self-esteem. At one level this seems to draw on the theories of Mead (1962) who argues that the self and in consequence self-esteem are created through the processes of social interaction. Those arguing that boys need male teachers seem to be saying that 'the significant other' must be the same gender. What this ignores is the way girls relate to male teachers and, more significantly, does not reflect the subtlety of Mead's original position.

In the past social psychologists have sought to relate children's self-esteem to the ways in which individuals identify with common toys. The most famous and controversial of these experiments focused on the identity of African black American pupils and later in England the identity of African-Caribbean pupils. The Clarks' famous doll test appeared to show that black children, in choosing a white doll as a playmate and as nicer than the black doll, suffered from low self-esteem. Subsequent repetitions of the experiment and the development of new methodologies have revealed that the picture is much more complex than the Clarks thought.

Nevertheless Bernard Coard's pioneering pamphlet argued that black children in England had low self-esteem, and what was required was powerful black role models and to be taught black pride, – in the slogan of the day that 'black is beautiful' (Coard, 1971). Later the work of David Milner in England challenged the simple view put by the Clarks but even so the need for black role models was emphasised (Milner, 1983). This sideways look at an aspect of multicultural education is important because it illustrates the way in which self-esteem, educational achievement and role modelling have been interconnected in a fairly simplistic manner. It is now clear that the causes and solutions to black African-Caribbean underachievement are more complex and challenging than thought in the 1970s. In fact current policy makers seem to be utterly unaware of the sorts of proposals put by Coard and others. Even more significantly, they seem to be equally unaware of Maureen Stone's powerful critique from the perspective of a black professional (Stone, 1981). Stone argues that concerns with self-esteem and role modelling turn attention away from the fact that what the children need is high quality teaching by skilled teachers regardless of who they are. This does not mean that the system should not be making every effort to recruit and retain black teachers.

The question of turning boys away from laddish culture assumes that the application of simple solutions will work. What is prioritised is the introduction of male role models and also appropriate ethnic role models. Policy makers make no reference to why boys choose to behave in particular ways nor do they have any sense of what boys actually think about their circumstances. This is the subject of detailed discussion in

Chapters 6 and 7 of this book. What we consider here is evidence from other recent research projects on what laddish culture means and why boys may choose this as an alternative to being locked into learning.

Laddishness

Perceived gaps in the average scores of boys and girls have been inextricably linked with issues of behaviour and discipline. We need to consider behaviour and discipline and their consequences. At first sight it would appear that laddish behaviour is easy to identify, but in fact this is not the case. What the then Secretary of State described as laddishness covers not just low levels of annoying rebelliousness and work avoidance but cases of extreme behaviour including long term truancy and even violence. The popular press regularly highlight extreme behaviour in schools, and it is to these reports that politicians regularly respond. It is worth noting here that a headline story is only such because it reports a rarity!

As with much we have to say in this volume more evidence and research has been ignored than considered in both the definition of the 'problem' and its suggested 'solutions'. The Secretary of State (DfES 2000) identifies the problematic boys group as consisting of 'underachievement among boys, particularly those from *working class families*. This underachievement is linked to a laddish culture which in many areas has grown out of *deprivation*, and a lack of both self-confidence and opportunity' (our emphasis). There have been good alternative explanations of the behaviour of working class boys and their lack of uptake of educational opportunities. The perceptive and controversial work of the Birmingham Centre for Contemporary Cultural Studies sought to make sense of behaviour that on the surface was counter-productive. While it is true that these studies focused on adolescent youth, they are relevant to the ways in which younger boys are described in the 21st century.

Paul Willis' (1977) pioneering study *Learning to Labour* sought, as its subtitle said, to show how working class kids got working class jobs. Willis shows that the lads' (rebellious or disaffected youths) behaviour had a different meaning for them than for their school: it was a reflection of how they knew they would have to resist the conditions of adult working class life. Hebdige's (1979) study of popular culture argued that youth style and varieties of music were forms of resistance to the pressures of a racialist and class-ridden society. At approximately the same time Peter Woods (1976) described and explained the nature of secondary school classroom behaviour, the function of 'having a laugh' in terms not of the teachers' but the pupils' meanings.

In contrast to the studies identified above, the behaviour and understanding of primary school boys is presented only from the perspective of adults. It is adults who have defined what is meaningful for them – football and action games but their voices are absent. Later we turn attention to what pupils, think, mean and understand but it is worth noting that there is a good deal of work still to be done on what primary school boys (and girls for that matter) actually think and function, and what this means.

Jackson (2002b) shows in a careful study of fifty boys in two secondary schools that laddish behaviour has different meanings for the boys than for teachers and others in the system. (She defines laddishness as a set of hedonistic practices revolving around having a laugh, disruptive classroom behaviour and an intense interest in masculine subjects such as sex and masculine games.) For us the critical point of her argument is the way in which for boys the behaviour protects from failure. In rejecting academic work they are insulated from the effect of failure/rejection. At the same time the behaviours are consistent in maintaining traditional masculine hegemony. The simple imposition of male role models would not and could not penetrate those behaviours since the policy takes no cognisance of the meanings and functions of those behaviours for their perpetrators.

Feminisation
A major role for schools is to create the 'good pupil'. The struggle to establish this pupil identity is and has been central to the

enterprise of schooling. This can only be accomplished by the good/moral teacher. Historically this was expressed in male terms.

> [The] conception of the moral teacher – a 'man' of character' – was fused with and filtered through other nineteenth century ideologies, namely. Evangelical protestantism with its civilising ethic, the revival of chivalry as a code for life and the 'race think-ing' of imperialism. (Grosvenor and Lawn 2001)

This conception seems remarkably similar to the vision of the good male role model striven for by current policy.

In Chapter 3 we show how historically the profession of primary school teaching has been a female dominated one. We also argue that the current policy initiative focusing simply on in-creasing numbers of male recruits ignores both historical and contemporary reality. The policy argument is confused in that for some years Ministers and their respective policy advisors conflate the gender make up of the profession with the issues of feminised and masculinised discourse of primary schools. In the case of primary schools it has always been the case that women were the majority of the work force.

Much social theory now rejects a straightforward notion of male and female gender roles and argues rather that we should consider explanatory frameworks drawing on the idea of feminised and masculinised discourse. This allows us to escape from simple role attribution. What we need to attend to is the nature of primary schools as organisations and the ways in which meanings are transmitted to pupils.

Even the most 'progressive' of primary schools are hierarchical organisations; liberal/democratic headteachers are still head-teachers. The management of primary schools is as centrally directed as the curriculum. For instance Ofsted procedures 'require' primary schools to show they have SENCOs, curri-culum co-ordinators, specified management roles for deputy-headteachers if they have them, and teachers responsible for child protection risk assessment and a variety of other things. Writers on management coming from a feminist perspective are deeply critical of these sorts of hierarchical roles. They argue that a feminised management discourse would be very different. The discourse of management for them is not simply one of control but a significant way in which meanings are transmitted, and pupil and teacher identities created and sustained.

Skelton (2002b) lists a number of features of that would contribute to a feminised primary school. For our argument the following are important:

- non-hierarchical management structure where decision making occurs on a democratic basis;

- more inclusive approaches to organisation of teaching and learning and correspondingly, less emphasis on individualism;

- school agendas that are informal and flexible.

It is argued that if schools had such changed structures the experience of pupils would be very different in that they would be subjects of a feminised discourse and that this has consequences for pupil identity and achievement.

How are primary schools managed? A cynical response would be: by central dictat and in response to heavy surveillance. We leave this cynicism aside to look at what is recommended to, and actually happens in, primary schools. Primary schools exist under a regime that is desperate to meet policy targets. The Secretary of State for Education sets targets that schools must meet to demonstrate their effectiveness and also to show that political promises have been kept. At least one reason for Estelle Morris's resignation was because primary schools had failed to meet the target that at end of Key Stage 4 80% of pupils would have achieved SAT level 4 in English. She was reminded of this by the House of Commons Select Committee and subsequently fulfilled her promise to resign.

Resign she did but that has not stopped the relentless target setting for schools in all aspects of their work. An important consequence of this is the reinforcement of hierarchical organisational principles. Teachers have to set targets in consultation with their management; in fact the targets are already set for both. It is ironic that the toughest targets are being set for boys. This kind of top down management is described by feminist critics as typically masculine, in that it creates a masculinist discourse of schools regardless of the gender of the local actors.

The headteacher is seen to be the key actor in the creation and maintenance of the successful school.

> Strong school leadership is essential to the success of all our schools. Good headteachers hold the key to unlocking the potential of pupils, all school staff and the school community. (DfES 2002)

This is the view of central policy makers, a view they have garnered from a variety of sources from the liberal to the less liberal management theorists. For instance, leadership is a key concept for Michael Fullan, a major liberal proponent of change and for the many contributors to business courses. The introduction of a new qualification in the 1990s, the National Professional Qualification for Headship, signalled a concern that the management of schools was not as effective as it might be. The introduction of the qualification, now a necessity for those wishing to become headteachers, required a definition of what constituted good practice. This practice is represented quite starkly by the standards to be met in order to be certificated. If we examine these standards in detail it is fairly clear that they do not meet the criteria that Skelton (*op cit*) sets out for a feminised discourse of management.

In the first instance, although there is some reference to team work and seeking advice, the majority are focused on the individual. The headteacher is the leader and the manager. We can set work as part of a team against two other standards:

* create and secure commitment to a clear vision for an effective institution

* prioritise, plan and organise.

The latter two place the head in the classic role of benign decision maker. In like manner the new head is enjoined to seek advice and support but only when necessary. The organisation of primary schools as projected by central and local policy makers is the antithesis of the kind of feminisation that recent theorists have identified. Are boys then simply reacting to an overweening surveillance and direction, not because it comes from women, but because it is the sort of pressure that needs to be resisted? Paul Willis' lads would surely be among the resisters, as would Hebdige's rude boys.

Male teachers and intending teachers

Although the TTA is concerned to recruit more men into primary teaching it has been reluctant to fund rigorous research to discover the opinions and perceptions of men. There is a common sense view that the current anxiety about male paedophiles, largely driven by the tabloid press, frightens men away from primary education. This is confirmed by Thomas Balchin, a junior school teacher writing in Forum, who comments on the problems men may experience in developing care relationships with children (see Chapter 2). It is difficult to make judgements about this since evidence is at best sketchy and anecdotal.

The situation in the USA is similar to that in England. Men in pre-school settings are rare and men in the equivalent of primary education form a very low percentage of the workforce. The rarity of men in pre-school led to a main article in *Education Week* in January 2000. It documented the work and opinions of Roberto Recio.

> 'Michael Jordan and the Bulls are part of Chicago, and part of the kids,' explained Roberto Recio, an imposing man who presides over a class of about 20 3 and 4-year-olds at Christopher House, a social service agency in an ethnically diverse, low-income community on Chicago's North Side.
>
> Mr. Recio, 33, is one of six men who make up twenty percent of the center's teaching staff. That percentage is noteworthy because nationally, men constitute less than five percent of the child-care workforce, according to *Childcare Information Exchange*, an industry magazine. (Galley 2000)

The major reason given for why men are so rare in the workforce is poor pay, but in addition men find it difficult to get employment because of fears of abuse and a widely held perception that women are better at caring for young children. These perceptions are also common in England. Skelton (*op cit*) surveyed student teachers to ascertain their perceptions of the different qualities brought by men and women to primary teaching. Men teachers held a view that women teachers have better communication skills and are generally more caring. What evidence they had for these views is unclear; they appear to be stereotypical. The fact that there is little evidence offered to support them is neither here nor there since these men obviously believe it to be the case and are therefore likely to act on it. Women students believe that men have significant roles to play in fostering good attitudes to study among boys and are needed as role models.

What Skelton's (2001) careful study shows is that even those beginning to engage in the profession hold views derived from common sense rather than evidence. Her colleague Bruce Carrington (2002) conducted a large scale study of male and female students' images of primary teaching as a career. All felt that primary teaching was suitable for both genders and that it was as intellectually demanding as secondary teaching. Seventy two per cent of men and 76% of women disagreed with the statement that women teachers are more caring than men. Carrington points out that his respondents are positively working against the stereotype that primary teaching is a female job and that what is required if we are to increase the number of men in the profession is to work against the stereotype. What primary teaching is about is not providing male role models but exciting teaching.

What we have set out is the contemporary context in which all primary school teachers work and the one in which student teachers also operate. Whilst it is a fact that the majority of primary school teachers are female, we now go on to show that this is neither a sufficient nor necessary explanation for the differences in boys' and girls' achievement and behaviour. We note also that the so-called gap is itself problematic. In the next chapter, we look at the problematic nature of primary teaching as a profession that embraces elements of caring as well as teaching. In Chapter 3, we consider the historical position before presenting, in Chapters 4 and 5, a theoretical framework for understanding the relationship between primary school boys and their teachers. In Chapters 6 and 7, we report on the research we have undertaken with boys, and in Chapter 8, on some work with teachers and mothers. Finally, in Chapter 9 we draw our arguments to a close with the conclusion that teaching skill and subject knowledge are considerably more significant than teachers' gender in developing boys' education.

CHAPTER TWO

Teaching, caring and Professionalism

Introduction

A small boy, aged about eight, is alone in the playground at lunchbreak. He is leaning against a wall, and a teardrop can be discerned on his cheek. How might we react?

1. This is a problem for the SMSAs

2. He's probably a sad case

3. He needs toughening up

4. It's my lunchbreak

5. I feel sorry, but he's not in my class

6. I need to log and report what I've seen

7. I'd like to comfort and help him

On the face of it, this might seem a straightforward question. However, it is difficult to avoid the fact that primary school teaching involves feelings. It involves teachers' own feelings as human beings, and the feelings of the small, vulnerable human beings they teach. Why choose primary teaching as a career? Within primary teaching, why a particular age range? Why teach in a primary school and not a secondary school? Answers to that question might well involve the nature of the curriculum. Many primary teachers do not want to teach only one subject all the time and welcome the opportunity to teach all the subjects. They may not wish to be driven by the GCSE exam, and might prefer to be involved with the all round intellectual and social development of children.

For some primary teachers, the children may well be a higher priority than the curriculum. That is to say, their first concern is with the children's welfare and rounded development as human beings rather than the need to develop knowledge of any particular subject. This might involve, perhaps at a private and deeply personal level, an emotional response to the dilemma with which we began this chapter. Primary teaching is thus defined as a caring profession. This possibility is perhaps more likely to appeal to teachers of younger children than to teachers of secondary age children who may gain satisfaction through imparting knowledge of their subject. Traditionally, in the United Kingdom, primary teaching has come to be viewed as 'both and' – a combination of cognitive 'subject delivery' and affective 'caring'. This chapter reviews the degree to which that may be a problem, and prepares the way for further discussion in the later chapters that review our empirical work with boys.

It seems probable to us that the present obsession with testing and results owes more to political pressure than to primary teachers' instincts and judgements as to what is ideal in primary schools. However, the balance between the caring, nurturing aspect of the job and the cognitive, subject teaching aspect needs to be carefully struck. It is by no means a simple polarity between child and subject centred views of primary education. Evidence from various pieces of research into school improvement does tend to suggest that children achieve most when teachers actually *teach*. This may sound an obvious truism, but what is meant is that the balance is in favour of cognitive subject delivery rather than caring.

As long ago as 1976 Brophy and Evertson found that in the most effective schools, teacher/pupil relationships were businesslike, task oriented and based on teaching and academic objectives. The least effective teachers were the ones whose primary orientation was to personal relationships and social objectives. (Brophy and Evertson, 1976). Long (2000), in summarising this and other school effectiveness research, concludes that the best teachers show that they care, not through a direct focus on the children themselves but by a commitment to helping the children with their work. This includes spending time and effort on careful preparation of work, differentiation and smooth management of classes, with little time wasted on behaviour or transitions.

This accords with our own view, which is that the best kinds of caring relationship with children are those that are based upon work undertaken in a calm, pleasant, but purposeful atmosphere. Such relationships are rewarding, but detached and lacking in emotional involvement. They allow teachers to show that they care through the degree to which they take the trouble to provide a calm and supportive atmosphere in which behaviour is well managed, *all* pupils can work, and the work itself is interesting and stimulating. We now develop this view before moving on to consider the considerable complications that tend to arise once the question of teacher gender enters the equation. In the final part of the chapter, we put forward our own recipe for successful caring in primary schools.

Caring and performativity

We begin this section with an exercise to help readers establish their own position regarding the balance between care for children and delivering subject knowledge:

View One:

Schooling is preparation for adult life. The purpose of schooling is to equip young people with the skills and abilities to function effectively in adult society, and contribute productively to the nation's economy. Primary schools lay the foundations for this.

Agree strongly 1 2 3 4 5 Disagree strongly

View Two:

Schooling is for the development of the person. The purpose of schooling is to meet young people where they are in order to develop their talents and interests. Primary schooling is a celebration of childhood and its creativity.

Agree strongly 1 2 3 4 5 Disagree strongly

Our experience of working with teachers leads us to the expectation that views are unlikely to be polarised to the extent of circling a five and a one. The argument that we would advance is that we get the best out of children, and do our best for them, when we strike a balance between the two extremes. To illustrate this, let us return to our tearful eight year old, with the request for a little empathy. Somehow, the eight year old needs to recover his composure and function effectively for the remainder of the day. How might he respond to each of the following?

1. He is completely ignored

2. A cold hearted adult tells him to 'pull himself together' and 'not be stupid'

3. An adult with whom he doesn't feel entirely comfortable gushes and fusses over him

4. Some children his own age taunt him

5. A couple of his friends try to cheer him up

6. He goes to a lesson which is interesting and stimulating, and begins to engage with it and even enjoy it.

Everybody is different and what works for one may be anathema to another. However, the research on which much of this book is based leads us to suggest that (5) and (6) are perhaps the most likely to enable children to become both fulfilled in their childhood and 'performing' optimally in relation to the curriculum. There is more to this than at first appears. We can give a low rating to (1) because children (people) are social beings and school is about socialisation. There are some exceptions, but the majority function at their best when 'socially connected'.

We can also give a low rating to (2). The 'pull yourself together' response may satisfy teachers' needs not to get involved, but is it really what anyone wants to hear when feeling down? It simply shifts the blame to the individual, making them feel responsible for their inability to be in control. 'Pull yourself together' is not the way to cure clinical depression, and neither is it the way to promote self-esteem and make children feel valued and cared for. Response (3) is undesirable. Unwanted attention can be embarrassing and make children feel worse. The balance of power between adult and child is such that we need to be really careful, remembering what it means to put children first. We have evidence that children do not like it when teachers want to 'know too much' about their personal affairs (see Chapter 7). A golden rule in handling children's emotions is that any action must be related to the child's needs and not any emotional needs the adult may have. There are many reasons for giving (3) a cautious rating.

Number (4) may seem obvious. Bullying in any form is hardly likely to make matters better. However, we must ask an important question. Where was adult authority when the taunting took place? What kind of school climate have the managing adults created that allows the taunting of a tearful eight year old to flourish? There is an extremely important principle here. In number (3), we see direct intervention by an adult. A positive response to number (4) requires indirect, structural intervention by adults. A particular kind of 'caring' is needed in this situation, and it is towards a definition of this kind of caring that we are moving in this chapter.

We would ascribe a higher rating to (5). Our research shows that peer relationships are by far the most significant to children in school, no more so than during the formative years of the Foundation Stage and KS1, when the principal focus of social learning shifts from adults in the home to age peers. Teachers whose motives for choosing primary teaching as a career were biased towards emotional caring as opposed to subject delivery may find this a little challenging. Children look primarily to their peers for emotional support, whilst looking primarily to their teachers for help with their work and an interesting, stimulating structure of intellectual and creative activity. The caring role of the teacher here is again indirect and strategic. Teachers are there to prevent the mayhem that erupted on William Golding's celebrated island happening at school. Their role is to patrol in the background, enabling children's relationships to flourish. It is not to participate in the relationships themselves.

Number (6) follows directly. It is difficult initially to focus on cognitive activities when the emotions are in turmoil. However, if the mind can be focused, it is often the case that distraction from the disturbing emotion rather than a direct confrontation with that emotion is the more effective. A sense of balance and proportion is restored, the original problem can seem much less significant, and the emotional intelligences as opposed to raw passion can function. A good teacher who is known for his or her ability to enthuse children with stimulating and enjoyable lessons can work miracles. Points (5) and (6) became abundantly clear in the recent screening by Channel Four television of the documentary *Boys Alone* in the Cutting Edges series (Channel Four, 2002).

In this programme, a group of twelve year old boys were left alone in a house for a week. They ended up by seriously falling out with each other and completely wrecking the house. One explanation that was offered for this was simply that the events vindicated Golding's view of the nature of boys. An alternative might be that the boys were given nothing to do, and thus suffered a disintegration of relationships in the absence of worthwhile goals. Caring adults are needed to manage children's relationships, and this is accomplished in the main by providing worthwhile goals and tasks for children to work towards. Unlike Jack and Ralph (the boys who quarreled over leadership in Golding's tale), the teacher has the advantage of standing *outside* the children's relationships.

There are sound theoretical reasons as well as research evidence for putting forward this view, and we discuss this in greater depth in the next chapter, which is about attachment behaviour. For the present, the following summary of key principles will suffice:

- The ultimate aim of schooling may be preparation for adult life but there is still a case for engaging with childhood during the primary phase

- A broad and balanced view of primary schooling would see pupils enthused by a stimulating and creative curriculum to which they relate as children

- Effective learning requires positive engagement of both affective domain (feelings) and cognitive domain in relation to both subject matter and social relationships

- Children perform best when they are happy and emotionally secure

- Emotional security at school is mostly dependent upon the quality of peer relationships

- Teachers have an important strategic role in ensuring that peer relationships flourish in a positive way

As yet, we have not mentioned the gender of the teacher. The view of caring that is emerging is of an indirect model based upon the oversight of children's relationships, in the main through their work, not a direct model in which the focus is upon relationships between teacher and individual child. Our view is that both men and women are equally capable of this kind of caring relationship, and equally capable of the kind of stimulating teaching that is necessary to secure the interest of both boys and girls. We do not subscribe to the view that women are inherently more capable of or suited to caring for children in school. Neither do we subscribe to the view that men are somehow inherently more capable of a rational, focused, cognitive 'subject delivery'. In theory, we are confident that the various prescriptions and proscriptions of primary teaching apply equally to men and women. Unfortunately, such a straightforward outlook on gender equality is complicated by the issues that we now move on to discuss.

Low status 'mothering' and 'poor men'
In this section, we are indebted to James King's influential study *Uncommon Caring* (King, 1998). From it we derive the terms 'caring *about*' and 'caring *for*'. What do these terms mean? Let us take some extreme examples, which are admittedly stereotypes, but usefully illustrative ones! Gandhi was a man. There can be

little doubt that he cared passionately *about* the Indian people, and that he did so in a way many of us admire for all sorts of reasons. He cared so much *about* the Indian people that, through his peaceful political actions, he changed an entire sub-continent. It is possible that he may have cared *for* some people that he knew personally or intimately, but this is not what he is celebrated for. He is celebrated for his grand schemes, and there is a tendency in history to associate grand schemes with male worldviews.

Florence Nightingale was a woman. As we know only too well, popular account portrays the way she cared *for* the soldiers of the Crimea. She dressed and bathed their wounds, probably soothing and comforting many troubled spirits. She is popularly celebrated as the archetype of the female profession of caring *for* – an intimate relationship with the individual. It is for this that she is celebrated, although to survive in the Crimea and confront the kind of prejudices and difficulties she over-came perhaps required certain qualities that might, in popular prejudice, be considered male.

There is a distinct gender hierarchy here. Caring *about* is male and high status, and caring *for* is female and of lower status. It translates directly into the organisation and work of primary school teachers. We can consider a popular stereotype in which the one male teacher in a school is the head. He is a very caring head, and he shows this in the way he carefully manages the budget, carefully appoints good staff, and carefully oversees the planning of an effective curriculum. No one doubts that he cares greatly *about* his school. Then there is the female recep-tion teacher. She is also a very caring reception teacher, and she shows this in the way she carefully wipes the children's noses, ties their shoelaces, picks them up and cuddles them when they are upset. No one doubts that she cares greatly *for* her children. It is the caring *about* function, however, that is awarded status.

Robin Alexander is brutal in identifying gender as one of the key issues that have lead to

> ....a primary teaching force whose education, training, social class background and gender combined to create a professional

culture of subservience and dependence. (Alexander 2000, p
144)

Given the degree to which the primary teaching force simply
caved in to a previous Ofsted Chief Inspector's campaign of
vilification, and the government's wholesale takeover of primary teaching methods, we are inclined to attach some
credence to his views. Were these events a consequence of
traditional, passive femininity? As already noted, far from being
totally feminised, primary schools are subject to a very masculine, hierarchical and technocratic management regime.
Feminisit writers such as Reay (2001) make this point and it
would seem that traditional feminity is under threat wherever
women aspire to more senior positions. The question thus
arises as to whether new wave feminist ideals of management
can ever challenge the dominant male model, or whether aspir-
ing female managers must inevitably foresake any feminist
principles they may have had. This is one face of the primary
teacher gender issue, the face which privileges and glorifies
men.

The other face, which sidelines and disadvantages men, has
been the subject of much attention in recent writing. Here, we
find that once again, common sense, mixed with liberal dosages
of popular prejudice and stereotyping is to be found where we
might have hoped to find sound, evidence based judgement.
The tabloid press in particular seems to have frightened men
away from primary classrooms through promoting a suspicion
of paedophilia entirely disproportionate to the actual evidence
of abuse. This is confirmed by Thomas Balchin, a junior school
teacher writing in *Forum*, where he comments on the problem
that men may experience in developing care relationships with
children.

> For those who care a great deal about the children they teach,
> it is very sad that they are pulled back from giving the best of
> themselves by this climate of suspicion generated by the actions
> of a tiny minority of people who have abused children. (Balchin,
> 2002)

It is difficult to make judgements on this, since evidence is at best sketchy and anecdotal. Nevertheless, the point we made in chapter one probably prevails here. If men *believe* or *feel* they may be under suspicion of paedophilia, they will act in accordance with such beliefs and feelings regardless of evidence or fact. This is particularly the case at the Foundation Stage and Key Stage One, where attitudes have changed since the 1951 government edict proclaiming that infant classes must be taught by women (see Chapter 3). Current government publicity does not really make it clear whether the desire is for traditional men who will discipline and teach subject knowledge to Y6, or for 'new men' who will undertake the more nurturing and motherly role of looking after reception and Y1 classes.

As with other difficult decisions, this matter seems to be left to market forces, and men must sort the problem for themselves. The evidence is increasingly that it is not easy for them. For example, Lewis and Weston report the comment of a male trainee teacher *'There have been two main comments I have received when I tell people that I want to be a teacher. They either call me a paedophile or gay.'* More alarmingly, they report prejudice by schools, as in this comment to a male trainee by a female deputy head: *'Her first instructions to me were all negative. Stay away from the toilets, don't touch the children in any way'* (Lewis and Weston, 2002). The *Times Educational Supplement*, however, having previously itself carried a somewhat irresponsible headline explicitly linking male primary teachers with perverts, saw fit to pontificate in a more recent editorial: *'But if we don't persevere, non-female primary teachers will become even more of a rarity, damaging children's education, equal opportunities and society in general'* (*Times Educational Supplement* 13/09/02 p. 22).

A consequence of all this is that a discourse parallel to the problem-with-boys discourse has arisen – the poor-men discourse. This is encapsulated by the following quotation from King's book:

> It's easier for women to be open. For a man to be sensitive and open with children, people see it as strange. 'Why is he doing this? Why is he always touching my child?' Whereas when women do it, it's OK. I'm not angry. I just feel left out and discriminated against because I can't be as open with a child as a woman is. (King, 1998, p81.)

Skelton has recently suggested that there may now be a growing division between what she has termed 'KS1 man' and 'KS2 man'. KS1 man tends to counter gender stereotypes, whereas KS2 man uses phrases such as 'Well, I've heard that.....' to put down KS1 man and reinforce the stereotype of the macho male teaching Y6 (Skelton, 2002a). There are thus two distinct issues of status in tension. For women, there is a choice between either remaining faithful to the traditional female ethic of caring *for*, or entering the world of masculinity and competing with men at their own game, either through the assertion of feminist principles or complicity with men. A failure to make such choices would seem to ensure that teaching young children remains a low status occupation for women, encapsulated perhaps in this confidence given by an interviewee of Foster and Newman: *'If you're a university lecturer you know your stuff, but if you're just teaching little kids basic words, you're not valued'* (Foster and Newman, 2001).

Behind this sentiment lies the clear prejudice that men are somehow more capable, both of management and of delivering rational knowledge. Male career paths might either fast track towards headships or university lectureships, or alternatively locate in secondary school teaching where subject knowledge unequivocally counts for more. When men teach in primary schools they, like women, must also reach a position of choice. Either they reap the patriarchal dividend and fast-track themselves towards promotion or they make a conscious decision to counter stereotypes and work actively toward the notion of the classroom teacher as a high status professional. There is also a third option of simply ignoring the status game and being content with one's lot, regardless of what may be written or said. This option would seem to be open equally to men and women who are unconcerned with promotion or what society is said to think about them.

Primary teaching as a profession is thus divided between those of either gender who are content with the status quo, and those who would seek, either for themselves or for primary teaching as a whole, enhanced professional status. The operation of gender in this dilemma is difficult to ignore. The stereotypes with which we have to work are those that define caring as female, and the disciplined delivery of subject knowledge as male. Given the relative numbers of female secondary teachers and academics, it is probable that more progress has been made in overcoming the latter stereotype than the former. It is the former that the remainder of this chapter discusses.

What kind of care?
How then to achieve a professional ethic of caring in primary education that allows men and women equality of opportunity to participate, and overcomes the damaging stereotype that caring for children is low status women's work? For this book, there is also the particular question of caring for boys. Are boys being disadvantaged relative to girls through being cared for by women? This question has to be asked in the context of frequent assertions of the common sense notion that boys who are brought up in single mother households need a male teacher as a compensatory role model. This concerns boys who are no older than eleven years. We must consider the nature of 'boyness' and the inadvisability of assuming that research findings that relate to adolescent boys apply equally to younger ones.

Reflection on the poor-men discourse reveals a fundamental problem. If it is true that female teachers sometimes hug and cuddle children (and by no means all do), then we must ask whether this is a *necessary* part of the job. We have earlier argued that the principal concern of primary schools is with learning, and that child care is incidental to this. Few would argue that even the youngest classes in primary schools are for child care first and learning second, but we are mindful of the fact that the age at which British children begin full time primary education is unusually young in comparison with many other countries. The desire to force formal testing and academic learning on children ever younger at the expense of play based methods seems yet another example of the masculinsation of UK primary education. We do not necessarily agree with it, but we must work with what we have, and that means accepting that once children start formal primary education, they are in the charge of professionals whose function is to promote learning.

Hugging and cuddling children would be a necessary part of this job if it could be demonstrated that it improved learning. Let us suppose, for a moment, that hugging and cuddling children is demonstrated to be a necessary part of the job – that children who are hugged and cuddled demonstrably learn better than children who are not. Let us suppose also that in a given school, there are two Y1 classes. One has a woman teacher, the other a man. The children in the woman teacher's class receive hugs and cuddles, whilst the children in the man teacher's class receive no physical contact. The children in the female teacher's class consequently enjoy superior wellbeing and perform better academically. This demonstrable inequality of opportunity would not be an acceptable situation. The logical responses would be either to employ only female teachers for young children, or to encourage and permit male teachers openly to hug and cuddle the children. It is a perfectly straightforward proposition, yet it is one that is fudged and glossed over in the current poor-men and we-need-more-male-teachers discourses.

The next chapter looks at the contribution of attachment theory to the development of a professional theory of caring in primary schools. For the present, it will suffice to say that attachment theory suggests that teachers' hugging and cuddling children is *not* necessary for improved learning. There is research evidence to suggest that a limited degree of appropriate physical contact may be beneficial in primary schools, and we summarise this in the information box below. There is a case that the kind of physical contact that is appropriate can be made equally by men or women. Some of the language that seems to be used in the poor-men discourse ('always touching'? 'stay away from the toilets'?) needs to be questioned. The issue of physical contact is a sensitive one. Various schools and LEAs will have their own preferred guidance. Our point is simply that such guidance cannot privilege women, and must be based on evidence of what is good for children rather than what the media choose to sensationalise or what men come to believe on the basis of anecdote and hearsay.

Research Box

Touching Children

Touching children is currently a highly sensitive issue, and one which impacts directly upon teacher gender as in the 'poor men' discourse. Generally, touching children is associated with caring for, whether the context be to protect from physical assault or to offer comfort and encouragement. On the whole, we have defined the role of teacher as carer about – one who manages relationships – as opposed to carer for – one who provides intimate personal care. However, we recognise that primary children are, to some degree, in a transitional stage between being cared for and the independence of adulthood. Some limited caring for, involving touch, might still then be appropriate.

Advice given by LEAs and schools varies, but errs overall on the side of caution. One major teachers' union advises its members not to touch children at all. However, this is the same union that has advised its members not to run school trips, and the motivation here would seem to be more the protection of union members from the litigation culture than the welfare of children. In this chapter, we argue that the standards or expectations with regard to touching children should be the same for all primary teachers, and that what is acceptable for women should be based upon what is acceptable for men. What do we know from research about touching children?

Child to child physical contact. The original attachment behaviour study, reported in Chapters 4 and 5, and the new study reported in Chapters 5 and 6 (this volume) both stress the primacy of peer relationships at school. In the original study, it was found that physical contact formed between 29% and 40% of the playtime social interactions of all boys in the school, but that the highest achieving and highest status boys had significantly more physical contact at playtimes. The difference was accounted for mainly by informal, rule based games rather than 1:1 interactions (Ashley, 1993).

Effects on work and behaviour of teacher to child contact
Although a small study by Heinig (1976) found no significant differences in reading gain scores between children touched and not touched, a systematic experimental study of five and six year olds by Wheldall *et al* (1986) claimed that *verbal requests, when reinforced by touch* or close proximity, were significantly more likely to be heeded. Averaged over the study, KS1 children who were touched spent nearly 40% more of their time working than control

groups that were not touched. These researchers also found that teachers are more likely to touch children of their own sex. Close eye contact and friendly holding of the shoulders were considered most effective and appropriate.

Children's response to teacher touch
A study by Neill (1991) attempted to identify the types of touch to which children responded positively and negatively, and the way this changed between young and adolescent children.

It was found that the perception of touch as sexual increases with children's age. There was very little touch in secondary schools, but younger children generally had positive responses to touch. Teachers did not have a privileged position over other familiar adults, and the 'rules' of acceptable touch did not vary according to the age and status of the toucher. Sex was a significant variable. Primary school boys preferred to be touched by men, but secondary school boys preferred women. The shoulder and arm were the most liked areas for touch, and the legs and chest least liked. Touch associated with praise or comfort was consistently liked, but touch associated with negative emotions was very strongly objected to.

• *Research seems to support the view that a primary school without touch is a school that deprives children of something positive and possibly quite important. Our view that men and women should be equal in terms of touching would seem to be supported in that the kind of touch that is appropriate is limited, not associated with emotional bonding or 'mothering' and certainly not with sexual activity. Primary boys' preference for being touched by men might be noted.*

From this, we deduce the following principles:

• Female teachers cannot be privileged over male teachers with regard to physical contact with children

• The underpinning principles must be based on research evidence of what makes for effective learning and children's wellbeing while remaining within the bounds of overall social acceptability

• It is possible to identify a theory based professional practice of physical contact that clearly differentiates between primary classroom practice and parenting.

• Hugs and cuddles blur this distinction and are unlikely to be appropriate, regardless of the gender of the teacher.

The task is to ensure that there is a professional ethic and discourse of caring in primary schools which is clearly different to the discourse of parenting. We wish to move away from any conception of primary teaching as 'mothering'. In so doing, we must equally move away from any conception of primary teaching as 'fathering'. Primary teaching is not parenting and any men attracted to primary teaching solely or mainly as a result of their experiences of parenting may need to reconsider. More than this, the common sense notion that the recruitment of male teachers is necessary as a response to single mother households needs seriously to be interrogated. The views of boys on this issue are examined in Chapters 6 and 7.

How then can we move towards a more professional and gender equal model of caring in the primary school? King's notion of caring *about* may hold the key to this. Caring *about* is essentially a management function requiring a degree of professional autonomy and judgement. This point emerges plainly in later chapters, which demonstrate that children do indeed have an expectation to be cared *about* rather than cared *for*. Suggesting 'management' may be implying a slight shift to the masculine, but this may be only a matter of interpretation. The need is to demonstrate that the teacher, as the main classroom professional, is different to the support worker whose role may be less strategic and more orientated to the needs of particular individuals.

Caring *about* can mean many things. For the classroom teacher, it can mean caring about the curriculum, which is a function which the present government has removed from teachers. Through this action, the government has contributed significantly to the deprofessionalisation of primary teaching and thereby, perhaps unwittingly, exacerbated precisely the male recruitment problem it claims to be trying to solve. It may well be that the restoration of professional autonomy to care *about* and manage the curriculum will make the profession more attractive to men. If this is not to be seen divisively and competitively in gender terms, the *women* teaching boys may have to exert pressure for the re-professionalisation of primary teaching in terms of curriculum management. This would include a visible female presence in demands for the restoration of a broad, balanced and creative curriculum. Women need to challenge the techno-managerial obsession with summative statistics, and if this means suggesting that such an obsession is the consequence of the *masculinisation* of educational politics, we would not stand in their way.

Caring *about* can quite legitimately mean caring about results, however. Not league tables but a genuine care and concern for children to achieve. Teachers have been criticised for having low expectations of children (particularly certain ethnic or economic groups). High professional standards of caring, related to the achievement of academic objectives, should not permit or tolerate low expectations. Such caring might demand, however, that primary teachers as a profession actively challenge approaches to assessment which they believe to be wrong. If teachers as readers and creators of research are confident that SAT testing is a misleading and inaccurate method of assessing children, then they have a clear duty as caring professionals to speak out and act on their principles. This is part of Robin Alexander's point quoted earlier. A professional culture of subservience and dependence is not a culture which ultimately cares about its clients in the way we expect of professionals.

For the classroom teacher, however, the most significant daily act of caring about children probably concerns the management of their relationships. Offering comfort to an upset child is caring *for*, and we all have this basic human obligation to one another. Caring *about* begins when it is realised that upset children may be indicative of professional failures to manage the social interactions of large numbers of children. Schools with bullying problems must rate as priorities for the development of more professional approaches to caring. At a curriculum level, this degree of professionalism is developed further when the responsibilities for promoting the spiritual, moral, social and cultural development of all children are fully appreciated and put into practice. There is simply no equivalent to this in parenting, and 'mothering' is a singularly inappropriate concept here.

Conclusion: the androgynous teacher

This chapter has argued against the conception of primary teaching as mothering. In seeking higher status for primary teachers as professionals, it has sought to counter the stereotype that teaching younger children is relatively low status work because it is 'only' an extension of what most mothers do 'naturally'. For men, there is a potential dividend in that they might have the opportunity of entering a higher status profession without risking the questioning of their own masculinity. This line of argument has revealed that the real issue is the perception of primary teaching as simply extended parenting. 'Fathering' is no more appropriate than 'mothering'. This leads us to the notion of the androgynous teacher who cares for children, not as a parent but as a professional concerned with high standards of teaching and learning, curriculum development, a professional approach to assessment and the ability to manage the social interactions of large numbers of children. Subsequent chapters consider evidence that suggests this construction of the androgynous, caring, professional teacher is the one that most appeals to boys.

CHAPTER THREE

The problem-with-boys in History

Introduction: Three centuries of laddishness

There is a current concern for 'good' role models and the assumption is that male pupils will respond, modelling themselves on appropriate males.

Connected with this is a view that there was a golden age in the past when there were more men in primary schools and as a consequence boys both behaved better and achieved better. Before turning to the question of the supply of male teachers it is important to remind ourselves of how behaviour and learning were perceived in the past.

Inspector Watkins reported to the Committee of the Council on Education in 1845 on behaviour in the schools he had inspected (cited in Silver, 1994). The minutes record his comments on a range of schools,

-   an ignorant school of disorderly children

-   little knowledge and no discipline in this school

-   altogether wanting in discipline

-   bad in all respects; master not qualified for a teacher; few and ignorant children

-   very bad school in all respects; children ignorant and undisciplined; master incapable.

Humphries' (1981) oral history of education at the turn of the twentieth century shows high levels of pupil disaffection, poor achievement and grave problems of indiscipline.

> The teachers couldn't control the kids, even in them days. They was proper little monkeys, all of them, not one no more than another. They did go to school in gangs and they did vent all their feelings out and the teacher 'ad a job to keep 'em down.

The reality of the past is that there was considerable disaffection and indiscipline. This seems not too far from the erstwhile Education Secretary's concerns about laddish culture and behaviour referred to previously.

> Tackling this laddish culture will be at the heart of the new strategy. The Government wants to identify the barriers to boys' learning, including peer group pressure, and ensure that there are more good male role models to challenge boys' resistance to learning. (Blunkett, 2000)

We can see that construing a sizeable proportion of boys as troublesome, anti-learning and difficult is not a new phenomenon. What has happened is a return to older concerns after a brief period in the late 70s and 80s of concern for the ways in which primary schools behaved towards girls and the consequences of that for future success. Her Majesty's Chief Inspector (HMCI) provides information in his annual report on the gap in performance between boys and girls, and claims are made that attention should be shifted to the performance of boys. In arguing for this case, a cause for supposed under performance has had to be sought. In searching for a cause it appears that commentators have suffered from educational amnesia. A glance at the tables of norm referenced tests used until the late 1960s to select pupils for grammar schools shows that girls had to gain a higher raw score than boys to achieve the same standard score. The explanation given for this at the time was that there was a developmental lag between girls and boys. Developmental psychological explanations have fallen out of favour and one explanation now offered is the 'feminisation' of the profession.

> The feminisation of the profession leads to an absence of male role models for many of our pupils particularly those from the majority of one parent families. (Millett, 1999)

Boys' underachievement has to some extent been attributed to the feminisation of the teaching profession. By feminisation is meant in the first instance an increase in the number of women teachers in primary schools as a proportion of the total work force. The evidence we have for this pragmatic definition arises from recent policy initiatives aimed to increase the number of men entering the profession as primary school teachers. For example the TTA (2002) is currently funding projects to increase the number of male entrants to training. This chapter considers the extent to which this process of feminisation has occurred and its possible effect on boys' achievement through examination of the historical record.

The early elementary schools

Clarke (1985) reports that in the 1830s reformers arguing for the establishment of infant education stressed the need for infants to be under the 'rule' of men. There is little evidence that the subsequent establishment of a mass system was driven by the same ideology. From the 1830s through to the creation of a mass compulsory system, pragmatism rather than gender ideology seems to have been the principle governing the recruitment and retention of elementary (primary) schoolteachers. Albisetti (1993) compared the composition of the teaching force in the USA and a range of European countries. He notes Patricia Schmuck's research published in 1987 as pointing to the increased opportunity, in the USA, for high wages and movement westward from the 1870s leading to 'school teaching (becoming) a good exercise for the young unmarried female'.

In like manner Evans (1992) notes that by 1877, a mere seven years after the introduction of compulsory mass education, women were 60% of the elementary school workforce and by the turn of the century 73%. In the early years of the pupil-teacher scheme a higher percentage of young men was employed but the pupil teacher scheme quickly became more popular for young women. The proportion of girls in the scheme rose from 32% to 46% from 1849-1859 (Rendall, 1990). This scheme and other opportunities for training permitted many women to become teachers and by 1914, women made up 75% of all elementary school teachers.

The teachers in elementary schools were working class or at most lower middle class. Teaching offered some stability in comparison to the insecurity of other trades. To more articulate members of the working class, elementary school teaching also offered the opportunity for some secondary education through pupil-teacher training. However, this education also fitted teachers for posts outside teaching which commanded more attractive salaries and the exodus of the men from the teaching profession was already an issue at the end of the nineteenth century.

Many working class women found teaching an attractive career. It offered a measure of independence and a respectable position amongst the employment which was available to them. Payment as a pupil-teacher provided many working class girls with the opportunity to stay in education and not be a drain on their families' finances. On the other hand, there were greater opportunities for working class boys with some education towards the end of the nineteenth century. As job opportunities increased, teaching as a career became less attractive to many men. It is also worth noting that restrictions on the employment of married women in England in the 1920s were aimed at opening up employment for young women, 'married women were not accused of taking men's jobs' (Oram in Albisetti, 1993). What the historical record up to this time in England and Wales clearly shows is that elementary teaching is viewed as, and in fact is, a job for women rather than men.

Becoming a profession

Teaching also began to develop as more of a profession from the 1870s onwards. Employment by a school board gave a teacher semi-official status and rates of pay rose rapidly for more successful teachers, alongside a more defined career structure. The building of large urban elementary schools required men of administrative ability as well as teaching skill and increasing numbers of teaching assistants. It was no longer the case that when you had trained you were expected to take up the headship of your own school. In addition, as elementary schools began to take on more higher grade work there was a demand for teachers with higher qualifications. Teachers began to take external qualifications and a few studied for external degrees. The period saw the establishment of training institutions and this mode of entry began to be prioritised. As this happened it became more difficult to recruit males through the apprenticeship route. Many school boards began to find difficulty in recruiting male pupil-teachers: in 1902 Nottingham apprenticed 23 girls and one boy and Birmingham apprenticed no boys for ten years after 1893.

Towards the end of the century, distinction between the pay of heads and assistant teachers grew. Heads would often earn three times more than an ordinary qualified teacher, but this also had an adverse effect on recruitment since, as schools became bigger, there were fewer opportunities for promotion to headship. An account of the London School Board at the end of the nineteenth century comments on how pay created difficulties in attracting the right quality of male teachers.

> It is somewhat remarkable that the women teachers of the board – speaking quite generally – seem to be people of more natural refinement than the men. And the explanation, no doubt, is the simple one that the calling of the School Board teacher is, from the pecuniary point of view, a poor one for men, though a good one for women (Wardle,1977)

The creation of local education authorities following the 1902 Act provided opportunities for further training in the new local authority training colleges. Status increased as teachers gained more qualifications. However, working class families often made great sacrifices for their children to become teachers. For example, many working class parents were worried about the changes introduced by Morant to the pupil teacher system and more systematic training to be offered, since the changes could seriously postpone children's wage earning potential. The number of pupil-teachers fell; in 1906-1907 there were 11,108 new pupil-teachers, but by 1913-1914 this number had reduced to 1691 (Dent, 1977).

Between the wars there were further moves towards professional development rather than mere training. Training colleges and university departments began to dominate education and training. The curriculum of colleges was broadened and student teachers were now expected to have some grip on theory, however elementary it might be. The Report of the Departmental Committee on the Training of Teachers for Public Elementary Schools chaired by Burnham in 1925 established more joint examination boards from the training colleges and the universities to take over from the Board of Education the responsibility for the qualifying examination at the end of the training college course. Thus by the 1930s the principal route into the profession was via the fulltime certificate course. This was seen as an important guardian of standards and professionalism. The opposition to the Emergency Training scheme set up in 1945 identified the dilution of the profession as undesirable and as leading to semi-skilled and 'ignorant' teachers. The emergency trained teachers were described by Professor Gruffyd as 'a vast horde of ill-equipped and ill-trained persons dumped among properly trained teachers' (in Crook, 1997).

Crisis in recruitment – the perennial story

Immediate after the 1939-45 war, schools like most other institutions of civil society, were in radical need of development and regeneration. They had been deprived of resources during most of the war and treated as convenient sites in which to deliver social welfare, for instance school meals. Lawn has argued that one important result of 'collecting savings and salvage, distributing clothes, milk and meals; working lunch-hours, evenings and holidays, the teacher felt herself to be valued and having a major role in the schools of a new education system, indeed a valuable place in the reconstruction of a new society' (Lawn, 1987 pp. 62-63). This enabled the recruitment urgently required after 1945. Before this could happen education needed restructuring. The 1944 Act passed in the year before the end of the war set out the structure and organisation of the new education system.

Alongside this, the McNair Report (Ministry of Education, 1944) discussed recruitment, retention and quality provision for the training of teachers. World War Two had hit recruitment in both mens' and womens' training colleges. In 1938 the Ministry of Education reported that 70% of teachers in elementary or secondary schools were women (Ministry of Education, 1945), and during the war many married women and retired women teachers returned to the profession. Educational reconstruction in the years immediately following the war was to be dependent on the numbers and quality of the teaching force. At the time there was a wastage rate of about 6% (12 000 teachers per year), and Colleges and Departments of Education were only producing 6000 – 7000 new recruits annually.

The McNair Report attempted to enhance the status of teaching to attract more recruits by widening the field of recruitment, suggesting measures to encourage children from secondary schools to stay on at school and also recruiting from industry, commerce and other professions. The Report also discussed enhancing conditions of service, which included improvement of buildings, reductions in class sizes, encouragement for married women to stay on, granting of sabbaticals, and giving the profession more status and general esteem. In brief, McNair was concerned to enhance the professionalism of teachers.

In terms of pay, the Report included comparisons in pay between teachers and clerical officers and junior executive officers in the civil service. Maximum pay scales were comparable between both male and female teachers and clerical officers, but junior executive officers earned considerably more than teachers, particularly should they gain further promotion in the civil service. The McNair Report thus concludes, 'The two vistas which present themselves leave us in no doubt that the scales are heavily weighted against the teaching profession' (Ministry of Education, 1944 p37).

However, with the severe workforce crisis in 1945, it became clear to policy makers and politicians that the system for training established before the war and its extension by McNair would not provide a teaching force as rapidly as was needed. As a result, the government set up the Emergency Training Scheme.

Emergency training was open to all suitable men and women. Suitability was defined in terms of personal characteristics rather than academic qualifications, leading to claims of professional dilution as shown above. It was originally envisaged that more men would be trained and it is still commonly thought that this was a major scheme for recruiting men. However, by 1947 it was evident that many more men than earlier predicted had returned to teach after the war and the rising birth rate suggested that more women teachers would be needed (based on the assumption that women were best able to deal with the needs of very young children).

Consequently, from June 1947, recruitment of men ceased and publicity was devised to attract women into teaching. Several emergency colleges for men became co-educational and between 1948-49 fourteen men's or co-educational emergency colleges became permanent women's colleges.

The success of the Emergency Training Scheme and the permanent training colleges and departments can be seen in the fact that recruitment began to exceed loss through retirement in the case of men in 1948, and in the case of women in 1950. In terms of numbers, at the beginning of 1947 there were 61,250 men and 126,250 women in primary and secondary schools; by 1950 these numbers had increased to 77 000 men and 132 000 women (Ministry of Education,1951). The larger proportional increase for men is worth noting here but the discrepancy was not a concern for policy makers.

Policy documents on teacher supply take this discrepancy in the male/female ratio for granted. Because of a general shortage of women teachers, the Interim Committee on Teacher Supply recommended in March 1948 that local authorities should impose a maximum quota for full time women teachers so that there would be a more equitable balance of women teachers throughout the country. This quota was continued in successive years (Ministry of Education, 1951). In the fifties it was considered that the supply of women was more urgent than of men. In particular, women when married were likely to leave the profession for family reasons and it also appears that because of marriage they were less mobile than men. The First Report of the National Advisory Council for the Training and Supply of Teachers (Ministry of Education, 1951) notes:

There has not at any time in the last five years been a shortage of men candidates for training, and even if the facilities for training were slightly increased we would not expect undue difficulty in filling colleges with suitable candidates. (Ministry of Education, 1951 p11)

The post war baby boom placed enormous pressure on infant schools and departments and it was assumed that women teachers would be needed to take these classes. Women were perceived to have the sort of maternal and caring instincts attributed to their sex and it was these personal qualities that were seen as essential for the education of infants. 'Nevertheless, the infants' schools and classes must be taught by women teachers and will be under quite extraordinary pressure during the next few years as a result of the high birth rate of 1946-47' (Ministry of Education, 1951 p12). The effect of using up the available women to teach infants had a knock-on effect. Men were generally only employed for teaching older children, 'in proportions which would not ordinarily be thought desirable' (Ministry of Education, 1951 p13). However, as the baby bulge passed through the infants, the Report acknowledges, the proportion of men holding posts for teachers of older children should fall.

In the fifties and sixties the department focused on the problem of recruitment and retention. What could be done to stop the 'wastage' of trained teachers, particularly women? The desire to 'dig qualified teachers out of the pit' has been a continuing theme for governments. For example, the Report of the National

Advisory Council for the Training of Teachers in 1965 advocated more training places for men at college, not because of the contribution which men might bring to primary schools, but to counteract the wastage of women teachers. Interestingly, the Report still repeats concerns voiced a decade earlier, that the results of increasing male numbers in colleges 'would tend to identify women teachers in primary schools with the teaching of infants. This might have a divisive effect on the teaching profession (DES, 1965 para 122). The Report also acknowledges, however, that the much lower wastage rates of men teachers should ensure that the junior and secondary schools enjoy greater stability of staffing as the proportion of men rises (DES, 1965 para 122).

In 1967 the Plowden Report (Central Advisory Council for England) returns to the question of wastage of women teachers. It complains of the enormous wastage of women and notes that women outnumber men by three to one in primary schools, contrasting with secondary schools, where the reverse appears to apply and men outnumber women by four to three. Two in five teachers in junior schools were men. Not all members of the committee saw this wastage as a problem; Molly Brearley, the Principal of Froebel College, regularly told her female trainees that the course would make them better mothers (personal communications with former Froebel students). Plowden showed quite conclusively that, with the exception of infant schools, men occupied the positions of power and responsibility and as a consequence received better salaries. While the number of male/female heads was roughly the same, reflecting the Infant/Junior school organisation common in urban areas, men occupied headships in Junior and Junior Mixed Infant (JMI) schools. In fact, more than half of male teachers held posts of responsibility as heads, deputies or graded post-holders, compared to less than a quarter of women (CACE, 1967 pp.313-314). The Plowden Committee put this imbalance down at least in part to the reluctance of women to apply for and accept promotion.

From the perspective of the Plowden Committee, an important reason for the difficulties in recruiting men in primary schools was the gravitational pull of secondary teaching where career prospects and conditions were considered to be rather better. Plowden notes that the 1944 Education Act limited class sizes to 30 in secondary schools, whilst simply reducing primary class size from 50 to 40 children (CACE, 1967 pp.320-321). Arguably, career prospects were and are better for men as there is a much greater chance of becoming a headteacher. Remember that colleges up until the early 70s offered infant/junior and junior/secondary courses and the bulk of the male entrants to colleges followed the latter.

The Plowden Committee was enthusiastic to note that more men were now teaching young children than formerly and that the number of male headteachers was rising. Making specific reference to the 97 'brave men' they discovered in infant schools, the committee notes, 'Some young children, particularly boys, may respond better to teaching from a man than from a woman, and most schools and communities benefit from the contributions of both men and women teachers. It is also clear that a staff on which there are men teachers is likely to be more stable than a staff made up exclusively of women' (CACE, 1967 p.324). This suggestion that boys may respond better to men is fleeting and as far as we can discern is the first suggestion that it might be helpful to boys.

In commenting on recruitment, Plowden points to a shortage of men entering training courses and suggests various reasons. Of the primary heads and assistant primary teachers surveyed, 65% felt that the status of primary school teachers was lower than that of secondary teachers. Moreover, conditions in secondary education were also perceived to be better: newer buildings; smaller class sizes; increased capitation allowances; more graded posts and chances of promotion all made secondary teaching more attractive (CACE, 1967 p.367). There was also a suggestion that undergraduates felt that teaching young children was insufficiently challenging intellectually. When Plowden appeared in 1967 only one primary PGCE course had been in operation for any length of time. From 1968 onwards there was a dramatic increase in provision.

Thus from the end of the second world war until the Plowden Report there was little concern about gender balance in primary school. Policy makers were concerned about ensuring that classes were taught and had scant regard for the sex of the teacher. And in the 1950s the gender crisis was about the recruitment and retention of women. The Plowden Report only gave fleeting attention to the issue of gender.

Looking at the workforce figures on female and male primary teachers since the end of the war presents some difficulty. The figures available up until just after the war refer to elementary schools rather than primary schools. This has the potential effect of overstating the number of male teachers because these schools taught children from the ages of five to fourteen This is further complicated by the way a number of large urban areas 'Hadowised' their schools before the war. What these urban authorities did was adopt a division between primary and secondary education, even though the majority of pupils in the secondary school left at fourteen. While elementary schools lived on until the middle 50s in many smaller urban areas and predominated in rural areas. Only with the introduction of nationwide primary and secondary organisation can we see what age phase teachers taught. It seems to have been the case that men were more commonly involved with the older children in all-age elementary schools. There was certainly a strong feeling in official documents that women should be teaching the very young, although the Hadow Report mentions that in Junior Mixed Infant schools they should ensure an adequate number of men (Board of Education, 1931 p.86).

The Hadow Report emphasises the demarcation between younger and older pupils in the primary school and recommends that 'wherever possible, the infants should be placed under the care of a mistress with special responsibility and special knowledge of modern methods appropriate to this stage' (Board of Education, 1931 p.56). Leonard Clark, in his memoirs, documents how at interview for a post as Assistant

HMI, he was asked 'if he knew anything about infants. This was a nasty one. How many young men of my generation could have answered this with any accuracy?'

In the case of the youngest children and particularly those in nursery schools and classes, official policy and the social context effectively excluded men. Indeed, men would have had great difficulty arguing for teaching the youngest pupils. The Report of the Consultative Committee on Infant and Nursery Schools in 1933 (Board of Education, 1933) identifies three main functions for the nursery school:

a) The medical and hygienic aspect which is primarily concerned with the physical well -being of children

b) The educational aspect and

c) The social aspect. (Board of Education, 1933 p103).

Given the standards of cleanliness of the day, many nurseries had baths and children were equipped with a towel, toothbrush and comb. The Macmillan Nursery in Deptford was very much concerned with hygiene and health. 'Children were expected to play outdoors all year and only had recourse to what was called the shed for bathing and in the worst of weather' (Macmillan nursery teacher). The Report goes on to outline the responsibilities of the headmistress of infant and nursery schools (note the term headmistress – official documents relating to education use the universal male pronoun 'he' and the noun 'headmaster', except when referring to the early years). In addition to general teaching duties, the headmistress would be expected to co-operate with medical officers, deal with behaviour problems and become the parents' adviser and friend (Board of Education, 1933 p.151).

Qualities of teachers of young children are outlined in several paragraphs. The first essential is that she 'should have the right temperament'. A teacher of young children should not only have a real love and respect for children, but should be a person of imagination, understanding, sympathy and balance. '...The possession of a pleasant voice is of the first importance: her manner of speech, her articulation, and her choice of words will serve as a model for the children who are learning from her how to talk and read...' (Board of Education, 1933 p.133).

Following the second world war, the Ministry of Education's pamphlet *The Nation's Schools: Their Plan and Purpose* (1945) again urged the advisability of separate infant schools if possible, so that the specific needs of infant children might be met and not submerged within schools where there were older children. It was stressed that these schools should be the responsibility of women. The 1959 Handbook continued to emphasise that nursery and infant teaching were necessarily the preserve of women. The female pronoun is used throughout and the Handbook states that

> A nursery teacher has to create an atmosphere which is serene and comforting. She needs patience and understanding of when to participate or interfere in children's doings and when to stand by or stand aside. Above all she needs a genuine affection for children and an interest which is something more than professional. She has to win the confidence both of the children and of their parents. (Ministry of Education, 195 p.29)

An explanation of pronoun use in discussing teaching older juniors is offered in an intriguing footnote. 'About 25% of the teachers in primary schools are men and 75% are women; women teach infants and usually the younger juniors, as well as some of the older ones. When the feminine pronoun is used here or the masculine pronoun later, what is said applies equally to the other sex' (Ministry of Education, 1959 p.59). It needs to be noted here that even in the late 50s and early 60s, only 25% primary school teachers were male.

Turning to the Plowden survey, we can see that although 45% of older pupils were taught by men, 90% of first year junior pupils (Year 3) were taught be women (CACE, 1967 pp.313-314). The Plowden Committee was concerned to a small extent with an increase in the employment of men to solve the instability in staffing seen to be the result of the high turnover of young women teachers leaving to care for their families. Rather than arguing for the specific ideological benefit of introducing male teachers in the earlier years of teaching, what was being proposed was a mode of ensuring staffing stability.

The 1978 Her Majesty's Inspectors (HMI) survey of primary schools examined 5,844 teachers, 75% of whom were women. Responses were sought from teachers of seven, nine, and eleven year old children. The gender of the teachers involved with these groups reflected the figures collected by Plowden and the figures available from the 1950s. Seven year olds were taught almost exclusively by women (3% men and 97% women teachers) – while eleven year olds were taught by nearly equal numbers of men and women teachers (49% women and 51% male teachers). In the survey schools there were 19% men and 81% women teachers (DES, 1978). Interestingly, by the time of this survey, the universal male pronoun is dropped to be replaced by a plural pronoun and teachers, deputy head and head.

In 1980, HMI replicated the survey for the five to nine year old age group (DES,1982), although the sample was much smaller. The 657 teachers surveyed were mainly women (90%). What can be seen here is that although being 75% of the workforce, they were still occupying their traditional role with the youngest children. Again, in line with the tradition of infant school teaching, all heads in schools for ages five to eight years were women; men held headships of about half of the schools for five to nine year olds (DES, 1982). Significantly, no mention is made of a need to increase the number of men in early years classes. There is no suggestion here of a gender crisis.

More recent figures for men and women as a proportion of the workforce are for the academic year 1999/2000 but these aggregate all schools in the primary sector including nursery schools and classes. The effect of including the nursery sector in the figure has a tendency to over emphasise the proportion of women. At the time of writing, the nursery sector is the domain of women. In 1999/2000, 16.7% of primary teachers were men; by 2001 it was between 13% and 14%. These figures show that the relative proportion of men to women in primary schools has altered over time. There is a slight decrease, but hardly the stuff of a gender crisis. The current situation is difficult to comment on. The Teacher Training Agency's (TTA) symposium on recruitment held in July 2002 noted that accurate figures for the gender of trainees were difficult to obtain because not all trainers kept such data. As discussed earlier, recent work by Carrington (2002) and Bricheno and Thornton (2002) throws into doubt the proposition that having more male teachers produces better boy behaviour and higher achievement. The only thing of which we can be certain is that, as in the past, men occupy a higher percentage of promoted posts than women.

It is clear from the historical record that there was never a golden age of male primary school teachers offering 'good' role models for boys. More importantly, as Watkins (*op cit*) and Humphries (*op cit*) show, there was never a golden age of discipline. It is worth emphasising that in at least one instance where Watkins found the children ignorant and undisciplined, it was the *master* that he noted as being incapable. This observation, dating from 1854, finds a parallel in our own observations in 2002. The ability to discipline boys is not quite the function of gender that some commentators over the ages have assumed it to be.

CHAPTER FOUR

Attachment theory as a basis for understanding boys in school

Introduction

In Chapter Two we considered caring as a central element of the primary teacher's job and concluded that it is both a contested area and a gendered area. We identified two principal conceptions of caring. Caring *for* was seen more in terms of an intimate, hands-on, one to one interaction with overtones of mothering and nursing. This was seen as lower status because of it association with unpaid work, and a less valued and less professional 'feminised' workforce. Caring *about* was seen more in terms of a management role in which the desire for children and schools to succeed was perceived as a form of caring, and the management of children's relationships predominated over direct participation in close relationships with children. This was seen as higher status because of its association with masculine styles of working and higher degrees of training and professionalism. We were careful to point out that women as much as men can and do participate in caring *about*, and that it can be problematic for men to care *for*.

Chapter 7 reveals children's views of caring, and reports on evidence that suggests that boys prefer teachers who care *about*. They do not have the expectation that teachers will form close emotional bonds with them and they do not perceive women teachers as substitute mothers or men teachers as substitute fathers. Chapter 6 looks at boys' views of teaching and shows that they expect teachers to perform a professional job in which the features of caring *about* predominate. These are conceptualised as helping you with your work and protecting you from bullying or peer relationships that are beyond your capacity to manage. Most importantly, boys do *not* differentiate teachers by gender with regard to this kind of role. Men and women are seen by boys as equally capable, or equally potentially incompetent. This indicates that where caring for children becomes potentially controversial through such aspects as physical contact, female teachers cannot be privileged over male teachers. This could mean less physical contact for women, rather than more physical contact for men.

Such a conclusion may be seen as controversial or even disturbing, and is likely to be contested by some teachers but applauded by others. A recently published study by Vogt (2002) confirms that there is no general agreement about this among teachers, and that attempts by schools, LEAs and government to legislate or guide on such matters as physical contact with children have not generally resolved the confusion. Vogt's study highlights the degree to which conceptions of caring are central to teachers' professional identity, but also supports the general direction of our argument. Vogt concludes that 'interpretations of caring as mothering, parenting and giving a cuddle are rejected by some teachers because they regard them as undermining teachers' professionalism' (p.262). This is contentious because it upholds what some might regard as a masculinised definition of professionalism, but it may need to be accepted for, as Vogt argues, defining a caring teacher as committed to teaching and to professional relationships with the pupils would allow caring to be valued without perpetuating the patriarchal discourses which destine primary teaching to remain a low status profession.

The problem with the discourses discussed in previous chapters is that none is grounded in a professional theory of caring and relationships with children. This is evident in Vogt's article where it is clear that the discourse is driven mainly by the personal whims and feelings of the teachers interviewed. The absence of such a theory from the professional training of teachers, both now and in the past, is remarkable. In this chapter, we attempt to underscore the principles described and argued for here, by reference to one such a theory. In so doing we demonstrate once again that women are fully capable of teaching boys, that the schools-are-feminised discourse is not a satisfactory response to the problem-with-boys discourse, and that the presence of men in primary schools is more likely to be justified by the society modelling argument.

The principles of attachment theory

Attachment theory was developed during the early 1950s as a response to the absence of a professional theory in relation to maternal deprivation. The World Health Organisation was concerned about the life prospects of orphaned and institutionally reared children, but no clear theoretical principles existed to justify the concern. The name John Bowlby is as seminally linked with attachment theory as Freud is with psychoanalysis. Bowlby's major works on attachment and loss are classics which underpin much of what is now accepted in the field (Bowlby 1952; 1969). Mothering and the importance of the close bonding of infants with their special carers is today accepted as so unquestioningly essential to children's thriving that it is hard to imagine that before the 1950s, there were no convincing scientific arguments to justify it. In consequence, many babies were reared, deprived of any intimate mother care, in large institutions characterised by rows of cots serviced by cold, emotionally distant (though female) nurses whose role was limited to the provision of basic physical maintenance.

Bowlby established that children reared in this manner were deprived of something that was essential to their thriving and later fulfilment as adults. He paved the way for the demise of these institutions and ushered in the way we now conceive child care. His ideas have been taken up by other later workers who have established further the educational links between bonding and attainment, notably Ainsworth (1967), Ainsworth and Wittig (1969), Winnicott (1965) and Heard (1978). These ideas, emphasised in this chapter, as well as work by Ashley (1993) have underpinned much of the ongoing work reported in this book.

Attachment theory is paradoxical in several ways, and elements of it are counterintuitive (as with many scientific ideas). The first and most significant paradox is that attachment theory is about *separation*, not bonding. This is not a difficult idea when it is realised that the ultimate purpose of early maternal bonds is to ensure that the person functions as a mature adult who is not reliant upon the attentions of a care provider. The nature of this process, and the occurrence of key markers and milestones along its course is surely a central professional concern of teachers. Teachers need, according to this theoretical outlook, to position themselves as key professionals concerned with the development of independence in children, and the successful separation of children from mothering. This professional goal does not sit comfortably with the desire that some early years practitioners seem to have to be substitute mothers.

The second paradox, however, is that there is a clear relationship between successful parenting and successful separation. In the next section of this chapter, we look at the difficult question of attachment behaviour as a pathology – in other words, what happens when children do not experience secure parenting. We show that this is undoubtedly one of the most problematic areas for primary, and particularly early childhood, education. In this section, however, we confine ourselves to the normal course of healthy development and we consider a third important principle: that what we call attachment behaviour exists in inverse proportion to learning. In other words, the more attachment behaviour there is, the less learning in relation to the curriculum occurs. This has the effect of giving weighty theoretical backing to the common sense notion that children who misbehave are less likely to progress in their learning than their peers. The significance of this should shortly become clear.

Fundamentally, what we call attachment behaviour is a repertoire of goal directed behaviours, the purpose of which is to promote an emotional bond between a child and a carer. Bowlby (1969) has established that there is no biological determinant that privileges females or mothers. The principal carer of a child can be its father or even another male. The important factors seem to be frequency and quality of interaction, which places the theory firmly on the nurture side of the nature/nurture debate. Winnicott (1965) has particularly emphasised the fact that attachment behaviour is a two way and reciprocal process. Both child and carer initiate and respond to the behaviours that promote bonding. In early infancy, cooing, grasping, crying and screaming by the child would initiate a response by the carer; holding cuddling, smiling, rocking and feeding would operate in the other direction. Bonds are established when appropriate responses are given by either party to these stimuli.

The educational significance of these reciprocal behaviours begins to become apparent when the child first achieves the physical maturity to initiate a new set of behaviours, known as *exploratory behaviour*. As the term suggests, exploratory behaviours consist of the child directing its attention to discovering things about itself and its environment, and are the foundation of all later learning. Crucially, attachment behaviour and exploratory behaviour generally seem to be mutually exclusive. Either attachment behaviour is operative and exploratory behaviour repressed, or vice versa. This is classically illustrated by the carer in the park scenario. A young child (perhaps aged two or three) is in the park with its carer. Seemingly oblivious to the attentions of its carer, it runs away to explore something which has caught its attention. Suddenly, it is for some reason frightened and immediately switches to attachment behaviour, running to take up proximity to its carer and signalling its distress.

Crucially to education, the stronger the bond between child and carer, the more frequently exploratory behaviour occurs and the less frequently attachment behaviour. This gives us another term: the *attachment state*. The attachment state is characterised by the *absence* of attachment behaviour. A child engaging in exploratory behaviour is thus in an attachment state. It does not have to exhibit attachment behaviour to re-assure itself that it is cared for, and can thus focus its attention on exploratory behaviour (or learning). Attachment behaviour exists to promote the attachment state, which, once achieved, promotes exploratory behaviour or learning. This has been confirmed in a revealing way by Winnicott's notion of *holding in mind* which describes the ability of a securely attached child to engage in protracted feats of independence and exploratory be-haviour through the retention of a mental image of the care-giver, with the expectancy of her/his future availability (Winni-cott, 1965).

These principles have been confirmed in clinical studies by Ainsworth and her colleagues, using procedures which might now be difficult to repeat (Ainsworth and Wittig, 1969). Clinical separation studies have looked at what happens when carers are deliberately removed from small children who were ob-served through one way screens. Although we might now ques-tion the ethics of this, there is no evidence of long term harm to the children who took part in these studies, and it was clearly demonstrated that the more securely attached children showed less separation anxiety, could tolerate longer periods of independence and engage more in exploratory behaviour. This leads to some very important questions. What can we expect in terms of secure separation from the normal five year old enter-ing primary school and to what degree do teachers take over the role of attachment figure?

To a degree, the answers are inextricably linked. However, we can say that a healthy five year old should generally be capable of holding in mind its attachment state throughout the school day. So most of the hours at school can be spent on exploratory behaviour. This is good news for schools, because exploratory behaviour, in principle, is learning, and most people would agree that is what schools are for. If attachment behaviour occurs at school, the child has lost its secure attachment state. This is seriously problematic because once attachment behaviour occurs, exploratory or learning behaviour will cease, and the attachment behaviour will persist until its goals have been achieved. In this situation, teachers may not know what to do. Some might be tempted to respond as a nurturing parent would to the attachment behaviour and might well cuddle or pick up the child. Others might label the attachment behaviour as attention seeking and apply the common sense (though scientifically unjustified) theory that attention seeking should not be rewarded.

Unfortunately, neither response can safely be justified. In the first case it needs to be understood that the child's principal attachment is to the mother, although it can be to the father or other primary carer. This has been clearly confirmed for the boys in our current study. The base line factor is familiarity and frequency of contact. Securely attached, successful boys will enjoy frequent contact with their mother, and this results in a bond that Bowlby maintained is qualitatively unique. It forms the secure base which allows the child to venture away on exploratory behaviour. Forming a successful working relationship with a new, less familiar adult (the teacher) is part of social *exploratory behaviour*, not attachment behaviour. A child who exhibits attachment behaviour at school is likely to have a less secure attachment state (i.e. carer bond). If a teacher responds as a parent would to attachment behaviour, the likely outcome is further confusion in the child's mind as to where the secure base is located. We therefore urge caution with regard to cuddling children at school on the basis of attachment theory, and point out that child/teacher relationships generally only last a year.

In the second case, however, there is an equal if not greater problem. Attachment theory suggests that it is not appropriate to label attachment behaviour as attention seeking. Attention seeking is not a scientific term in the sense that attachment behaviour is. It is an everyday judgmental term used by teachers and others whose work involves them with children. According to attachment theory, attachment behaviour is goal directed and will persist, with increasing intensity, until the goal is achieved. To label attachment behaviour as attention seeking and ignore it will not result in its going away. It will result in increasingly pathological forms of attachment behaviour, to which we ascribe labels such as disruptive or deviant. The disruptive child's attention seeking, therefore, is a justified need. There is a conflict here between two theories. Behaviourist theories might claim that the rewarding of attention seeking acts as a reinforcer for that behaviour. We rest our case on the fact that there are many unfortunate children in our schools whose constant attention seeking is extremely disruptive, and for whom behaviourist approaches offer at best containment.

There are clearly great dilemmas for teachers here, and we discuss the difficulties further in the next section on attachment behaviour as a pathology. However, there is first one final piece of the attachment theory jigsaw to be added. The relationship of the child with the teacher is an ongoing part of social exploratory behaviour rather than an attachment state. In other words, the child is not forming a permanent emotional bond with the teacher, but is *learning* about relationships in the wider world. Teachers are clearly very important people because of the lessons they give children about adults outside the family. If this is true for teachers, then what of children's own peers? Bowlby's work indicates that the attachment bond with the principal parent is unique and qualitatively different to any attachments that might form to peers. Peer relationships, however, are also of a different qualitative order to child/teacher relationships, and form the final vital part of the puzzle.

Peer relationships form as a result of social exploratory behaviour. The child learns, through social experimentation, that some children are fun or rewarding to be with, others are boring, yet others are hostile or negative in affect. This is a hedonistic view of social learning in which individual, personal pleasure or satisfaction is the motivator. It is, nevertheless, a view which seems justified by our evidence. Thus children associate with other children who enhance their sense of social wellbeing. Unlike the majority of teacher associations, however, these peer associations often endure for longer than the school year. Sometimes they last for a child's whole primary school career and into secondary education or even beyond.

Gradually, through the continued attrition of social learning, early hedonistic conceptions begin to mature as moral codes of friendship are discovered and invented. The successful child learns, through this protracted process, the 'rules' for successful relationships and heads slowly in the direction of social altruism.

The peer attachments developed through this process are qualitatively different to parent/child attachments, and different again from any passing feelings of loyalty or affection a child may have for a particular teacher. They are not true attachments in the sense of a maternal bond, but might rather be seen as a developmental learning stage as the child journeys towards adult partner bonding and the eventual bonding with any children that might result. The ability to form cohesive working relationships and friendships with others is part of the process, as is the developmental learning of the moral and social principles that govern such relationships. A particularly remarkable and enduring feature of peer relationships during the primary education phase is the degree to which they are same sex. Although this obvious observation has been widely recognised for decades, surprisingly little is understood about the process. Gender studies are only now fully exploring the way in which boys and girls develop masculinity and femininity through social construction processes, and why same sex relationships seem to characterise the primary phase years to the extent they do.

However, peer relationships are considerably more significant than child/teacher relationships in determining the outcomes of schooling. The influence of peers is much more significant in determining the emotional state with which a child approaches learning than is supposed by authors who focus only on the teacher. By the time children reach Key Stage Two, peer relationships have assumed greater significance than teacher relationships as determinants of children's attitudes and values. It is perhaps for reasons such as this that the problem-with-boys discourse has assumed such proportions. There is an uneasy feeling that when boys refuse to work because peer culture

Research Box

In this box, we present some key research summaries which support our general contention that peer relationships are more significant than teacher/ pupil or 'role models' in the development of the kind of attachments that generate attitudes amongst primary school children.

Emma Renold (2000) makes the key point that very few ethnographic studies locate the primary school as a key arena for the production of sexual identities. In a later paper (Renold 2001) she reports on a detailed study of sexualised bullying and harassment amongst Y6 primary children. She did not find the innocence that might be presumed. Instead, there was much evidence of boy on girl and girl on boy harassment, much of it related to the promotion by both boys and girls of hegemonic, heterosexual gender relations. Peer relationships were found by Renold to be a key arena for the construction of attitudes, from which teachers were significantly excluded. A lengthy extract of an interview with two girls, for example, makes it clear that the problem of boob punching and bra pulling they are experiencing is not for teachers. The teachers, they feel, would not in any case take it seriously.

A detailed ethnographic study by Simon Pratt (2000) confirmed the importance of male friendships. Physical attractiveness and personality were the most significant features in choosing friends. Shared interests and the possession of an admired skill were also significant. Boys did not like bad behaviour in school and would not choose as friends boys who swear, fight or disrupt lessons. Friendship bonds were primarily non-reciprocally based upon personal gain. Few boys saw the friend gaining something from the friendship. These findings closely mirror the ethnographic study undertaken by Ashley between 1988 and 1992. Pratt also found that boys talked to each other a good deal, which conforms with the more recent research undertaken for this book. Subjects of talk included computers, games, trips, holidays, going to secondary school and football. Mention was also made of 'secrets'. Pratt highlights the orthodoxy that there is low self-disclosure amongst boys. It is interesting that here the supposed female trait of high self-disclosure and talk of relationships is posited as the norm, males being seen as deviant. More conventional gender positioning might have it that females are deviant because they talk excessively about personal things and relationships.

Diane Reay (2002) has published the case study of Shaun, a white working class boy struggling with the 'psychic work' of maintaining the twin personae of a hard, fighting lad and a boy working to achieve at school. The meticulously detailed study traces Shaun's progress from Y5 to Y8 and tells of how his hopes of doing well at school (see Chapter Five of present volume) are dashed by going to Sutton Boys' School – one of New Labour's 'sink schools'. The account tells not the conventional story of a boy struggling to separate from his mother in order to identify with a heroic male role model father, but of a boy who 'admires his mother more than anyone else in the world' and who thinks his black, female teacher is 'just brilliant'. The association between female parent attachment, respect for a female teacher's ability and a boy's desire to achieve is notable, as is the dire situation created by a sink all boys' school and failed male role models (Shaun's father was banned from seeing the children for, amongst other things, cutting up Shaun's sister's pet rabbits). Again, this story conforms better with our own evidence than do conventional accounts of masculinity. The damaging emotional inadequacy of the all boys' school might be compared with the well known account by Askew and Ross (1988), and a recently published study by Lovegrove (2002) in which an all boys' school compares unfavourably with several other schools with regard to bullying and harassment associated with personal appearance.

Hickey and Fitzclarence (2000) have recently made a strong case in which the effects of primary school boys' social groups and older teenage boys' groupings are compared. They cite Harris (1998), a developmental psychologist, who argues that peers matter much more than has been recognised in the past, and that adult role models matter less. This is as much the case for 'little boys' as adolescents. In their narrative 'Little Boys', Hickey and Fitzclarence relate how the values and attitudes of seven and eight year old boys were developed through football based peer interactions at playtimes, and not by the teacher or school. The attitudes that were developed could be described as hegemonic male ones of sport worship and female put down. The female teacher had not engaged with what was going on outside her lessons, and the boys consequently were not in receipt of any feminine moderating influence on their aggressively all-male playtime behaviour. This again conforms with our own observations and points towards the need for active feminine influence, rather than a male teacher who might only reinforce the playtime attitudes (see Skelton 2001, 126-129).

declares work to be 'uncool', a situation may exist that is getting out of hand. To hope that a small increase in the proportion of male primary teachers might somehow address these issues is a fatuous, irrational and even despairing response which largely ignores all the principles and observations discussed here.

It is not a counsel of despair to assert that peer relationships not teacher relationships are the dominant force in primary education. It is perfectly possible for teachers and schools to work *with* this principle, and the remainder of this chapter shows this can be very empowering. A good starting point is the finding reported in Chapter 6 that the majority of boys interviewed in our present study did not agree with the work-is-uncool idea. Most significantly, however, we believe that attachment theory as described in this chapter supports the principle of caring *about*. During primary education, children learn attitudes and values and develop socially and morally through what is described in this chapter as social exploratory behaviour. The teacher who cares *about* children will understand and work with this process. In the next chapter, we suggest how. But first attachment behaviour is considered as a pathology. This is necessary because the existence of pathological attachment behaviour sets limits to what is possible, and teaching is not a profession known for clear limits to the expectations of what teachers can realistically deliver.

Summary

- Children do not form emotional bonds with teachers in the way they do with their carers at home

- Primary teaching is not 'mothering' and clear professional boundaries need to be drawn

- An emotional bond between a child and its principal carer at home provides a *secure base*, which is the springboard for learning at school

- Peer relationships develop as a result of social exploratory behaviour

- Peer relationships increasingly govern children's attitudes to learning

- The most effective way for primary teachers to care is through the oversight of peer relationships

- The sex of the teacher is largely irrelevant when professional caring is so defined

- Attention seeking or disruptive behaviour may be attachment behaviour which has failed to achieve its goal, and this is problematic.

CHAPTER FIVE

Attachment Behaviour as a theory of caring and teaching

Introduction

The principles of attachment theory have been established as viable. Attachment theory can inform the two most fundamental functions of the primary teacher: developer of knowledge, skill and understanding, and as carer. Attachment theory is attractive, not only because it is elegant and successfully accounts for observed phenomena but also because it unifies these two main functions. It does this through postulating an inverse relationship that is of fundamental importance. Knowledge, skills and understanding develop as a result of exploratory behaviour. Exploratory behaviour occurs in inverse proportion to attachment behaviour. When all goes well, teachers can focus on the development of knowledge, skills and understanding because attachments formed in early infancy result in a secure base that allows a child to develop socially and to function successfully as a learner. This social development occurs mainly through peer attachments, which are crucial in determining the level of secure base upon which the child's learning depends.

When things go wrong, however, teachers are confronted by attachment behaviour, which makes inappropriate and often impossible demands in terms of caring, and largely closes off the routes to learning through exploratory behaviour. This chapter illustrates some of these principles in practice. First, we look at the idea of attachment behaviour as a pathology, what happens when children fail to form peer attachments, a situation that is not helped by some teachers' stereotyped expectations of the behaviour of boys. Then we look at a case of successful learning which is based upon strong peer attachments. It emerges that in both cases, the concept of caring through the act of class management and an applied interest in the curriculum are the crucial factors. The teacher who is seen to have the qualities required for this kind of caring is portrayed as potentially much more successful than the teacher who perceives her role more in terms of a substitute mother.

Attachment behaviour as a pathology

The principles described in the previous chapter rely on the assumption that children will have a secure base at home. Unfortunately, as any experienced primary teacher will testify, this is not the case for all children. Children who do not have a secure base at home are likely to be troublesome at school. The troublesome behaviour that results from the lack of a secure base ranges on a continuum from withdrawal to aggressive defiance, but is generally associated with poor attainment. This is exactly what we would expect from attachment theory, because attainment is linked to exploratory behaviour, which exists in inverse proportion to attachment behaviour. The child who lacks a secure base will perform attachment behaviour in an attempt to achieve one. This is manifest as disruptive attention seeking and a lack of on task learning behaviour. Many teachers' instincts are to ignore the attachment behaviour and to chastise the child for the lack of on task learning behaviour. This results in intensification of the attachment behaviour which takes increasingly deviant forms. This is when attachment behaviour is a pathology.

This is a difficult situation to deal with. The child performing attachment behaviour actually does need attention. Attending to that child's needs will result eventually in attainment of the goal of attachment behaviour – the attachment state, which allows exploratory or learning behaviour to take place. Unfortunately, as we have suggested, teachers are not the appropriate people to do this, and need to resist the temptation to substitute for inadequate parenting.

As any teacher who has tried will know, attending to the needs of children who lack a secure base is extremely time consuming. Such children are quite damaged and require a huge amount of attention and caring *for*. As far as schools are concerned, this is the point at which a clear professional and occupational boundary can be drawn. Attachment theory ought to justify schools calling in other professionals and stating clearly that it is not a teacher's job to intervene or feel responsible when parenting has been inadequate. This is the first part of our response to attachment behaviour as a pathology – simply to grant it legitimate recognition and use it as a means of limiting the professional demands made of teachers. However, there are things that teachers can and perhaps should do in their classroom management role as carers *about*, and these are now described.

There is no moral or political imperative for any particular form of secure base. Attachment theory does not privilege the 'ideal' two parent heterosexual nuclear family so beloved of the moral right. As we have seen, the operative factor is frequency and quality of contact. The principal home carer can equally be male or female, and the secure base can rest with one or two adults at home in varying proportions. This is extremely important, because it challenges another popular myth of the problem-with-boys discourse – that of the absent father. There appears to be little evidence that supports the idea that boys growing up in single mother households need to have a compensatory male role model in school. Indeed, rather sadly, our evidence often suggests the contrary. A poor male role model at home or school can do a great deal of damage, whereas no male role model at all does not necessarily lead to any kind of problem.

What happens if a child comes to school without a secure base at home? Jake, one of the boys studied in depth in the original ethnography, answers this question and points to things that the teacher should do in caring *about* the performance of boys.

Jake did not have a secure base at home when he started school. Unfortunately, as far as could be determined, a poor male role model had something to do with this. When Jake started school, he performed attachment behaviour. The teacher he was placed with could have responded by giving him attention of the kind that might have included hugs or cuddles. What the observed outcome of this would have been on Jake's subsequent school career is not known. What is known is that Jake's teacher responded by publicly labelling the attachment behaviour as deviant and undesirable. A clear message was given to the other children that Jake was a 'very naughty boy' and they should avoid him.

Immediately, negative expectations were set in motion for both teacher and children. The children responded to these expectations and began to construct interpretations of Jake's behaviour that conformed to the expectations and reinforced the behaviour. Thus rough and tumble play by Jake was constructed as hostile, whilst rough and tumble play by popular boys was constructed as fun. Jake's needs for positive affirmation were not met and an escalating cycle of pathological attachment behaviour was firmly set in place. It is significant that Jake's teacher was rejecting of him. It is considerably more significant that Jake's peers rejected him, and *were encouraged to do so by the lead given by the teacher.*

When Jake was in Y4, extensive data on the children's social behaviour were gathered. The five most disruptive children in the school (all boys, and of whom Jake was one) were first identified through a process of teacher consultation. A contrasting group of five academically successful boys and a third random control group were then identified. Each of these boys was systematically tracked on a rota basis over two school terms. Using methods derived from ethology (Lorenz, 1937; Harlow and Harlow, 1971; Blurton-Jones, 1974) every playground interaction of the target boy was observed, classified and mapped against a large database of the social relationships of all the 240 or so pupils in the school. Extensive use was made of sociometric testing and mapping. Detailed interviews were conducted to ascertain the attitudes of the other children and teachers towards the target children. An analysis of reported attitudes and observed behaviours was undertaken. These data were compared with teachers' reports of classroom behaviour and a range of data on academic performance.

No evidence could be found in this study to support the notion that the successful boys had more secure or better attachments to their teachers than their less successful peers. The successful boys and their teachers seemed to enjoy pleasant working relationships, but at the same time the boys made no emotional demands of their teachers and passed from one year's teacher to another without any symptoms of concern. However, examination of the peer relationship data revealed a very different picture. There were extremely strong relationships between the quality and quantity of peer relationships and the academic performance and classroom behaviour of the boys, none more so than Jake.

Three types of peer attachment were identified. The first type consisted of boys who had strong peer attachments and performed well at school. These boys were either 'sociometric stars' who exerted considerable influence on the pattern of social relationships, or they were less extrovert boys who nevertheless enjoyed strong attachments which were reciprocated by the social stars. These boys had strong attachments in their own group, and were also generally liked by the other children. The second type consisted of boys who had strong attachments to a smaller group of other boys. These boys were likely to be either disruptive or generally anti-learning in their attitude. They enjoyed good relationships in their own group, but were disliked by the majority of other pupils. The third type consisted of boys with no strong attachments or group identity. These boys tended to be moderate to indifferent performers academically, and were not highly visible in the general milieu of social relationships.

Teachers were found to have little positive influence on these groupings but a strong negative influence. One of the most potent acts a teacher could perform was found to be the reinforcement of children's dislikes of the already unpopular children. Negative interactions, in general, were much more potent than positive interactions. The qualitative evidence confirmed that children's positive choices of friendship were based upon hedonistic and selfish considerations. For example: *'He lets me go to his party sometimes'*; *'When people try to beat me up he stops them'*; *'He gives me sweets if he has leftovers'*; *'When I invite him he always does what I want'*; *'He helps me draw things.'*

This was echoed strongly in the quantitative data, where it was found that negative interactions in the playground were much less frequent than neutral or positive reactions, but at the same time had much stronger and more enduring influences on behaviour. In other words, a neutral or positive interaction would pass off as part of daily existence, whereas a negative interaction significantly disturbed emotional wellbeing, was remembered and recalled for a long time, and considerably influenced the individual's expectations and interpretations of the behaviour of the originator of the negative interaction.

Jake's case was particularly illuminating in this respect:

Effects of Contact

	Pos.	Neu.	Neg
High status mean	21.3	76.4	1.9
Low status mean	25.9	70.1	3.5
Disruptive mean	19.3	70.8	9.2
Jake	**4.1**	**72.4**	**22.8**

How could things have been different? How should teachers respond in cases such as this? It has to be stated that when Jake came to me as a pupil, I responded by offering him warmth, comfort, and affirmation which included some appropriate physical contact. I was able to develop a relationship with him, and his behaviour in my class improved. I recall interviews with his parents. On one occasion his mother burst into tears as she described her difficulties with him at home. On another occasion his stepfather came into school and said that at last there was a teacher who understood Jake and could offer a new beginning. My justification for my actions at the time lay in attachment theory. I believed that if I responded to his attachment behaviour, it would decrease and a secure base would be established. Some apparent success was achieved, although reviewing the situation over fifteen years later I tend now to place a different interpretation upon it.

Jake's story could be interpreted in support of the more-male-teachers discourse. As reported in the next two chapters, several of the boys we interviewed tended to suggest that a man would understand them better. Here indeed was a man, at last understanding Jake, forming a relationship with him and improving his behaviour. I do not have long term data on Jake and I am unable to say what happened to him subsequently. More significantly, however, I now acknowledge that there was other work I did with the class. For example, I vigorously countered negative labelling, I ran circle times when children could openly discuss their feelings, I constantly counseled the class that Jake had a good side and really only wanted friends, I intervened to protect the children from negative experiences of Jake's behaviour through running supervised lunchtime activities. I succeeded in reducing the quantity of negative encounters that the other children had with Jake, and I now believe that it was this, rather than my personal relationship with him that most influenced any improvements in his behaviour. Whilst I imagined I was caring *for* Jake, I was actually caring *about* the whole class.

Two crucial points emerge. The first is that I did not do anything that only a man could have done. Women are potentially at least as capable of running circle times and countering negative labelling. The second is that, although a male, I was in touch with what some people would call my feminine side. My response to Jake was not to 'have a kick around' with him as the macho footballing male role model might, but to emulate what a good woman teacher who cares *about* her class would do. On that, I rest my case. Perhaps the final word should go, however, to an interesting study by Barrett and Trevitt (1991), who hypothesised that remediation of learning difficulty was possible through an educational 'attachment figure'. These authors reported some success with this principle, describing positive outcomes in English schools with 'learning disabled' boys aged between seven and sixteen. In these cases, the 'attachment figure' was a therapist. Unlike the class teacher, the therapist had the time and training to fulfil this role. Perhaps the case should rest there.

Summary

- Attachment behaviour can be pathologised as negative attention seeking when the need for a secure base is not met

- When faced with disruptive, attention seeking behaviour, teachers need to target their caring skills at the whole class rather than to focus only on the individual

- Some children may have emotional needs teachers cannot meet, and boundaries need to be drawn

- Schools are fully justified in calling in other professionals when children lack a secure base resulting from inadequate parenting

- The sex of the teacher is largely irrelevant when professional caring is defined

- Male teachers may need to be in touch with their feminine (i.e. emotional) side

- Female teachers may need to be in touch with their masculine (i.e. management) side and curtail their mothering instincts

Attachment theory and successful learning

This final section considers the influence of peer relationships in the case of Peter. Peter was a successful male role model for boys in a primary school. He was eight years old when this observation was recorded. Peter was the central sociometric star of his class, and undisputed leader of what was termed in the study 'the football crowd'. Readers unfamiliar with sociometric testing will need to understand that the children had been asked to nominate, by secret ballot, whom they would like to share a room with on a forthcoming school trip. They were also asked to nominate any children they would not like to be with on the trip. They were later interviewed individually about their choices, and their choices were also cross referenced against a computer database of playground observations, which allowed a check to be made on whether theoretical choices could be observed in practice as genuine playtime associations. The results are described in detail in Ashley (1992).

On the basis of these data, it can be confidently asserted that Peter was the most admired boy in the class. Playground observations revealed that Peter ruled the large group of boys who dominated the frequent takeovers of the main part of the playground by the football crowd. Nearly all the boys in the class wanted Peter as one of their friends on the school trip. Significantly, it was found that Harry and James, the two boys who came second and third in popularity, were best friends of Peter. In the sociometric test, their friendship choices were 100% mutual. Each nominated each of the others in the secret ballot. Lower status boys also nominated Peter as their friend, but were not reciprocally nominated by Peter. Playground observations confirmed this pattern. Peter, Harry and James enjoyed close bonds and formed part of the in-group at the core of the football crowd. Lower status boys appeared to have idealised or fantasy friendships with Peter. They would say in interview he was their friend, but this was not confirmed by observation or by Peter.

Peter was undoubtedly a talented all round sport player, certainly a boy to be admired for his 'skill' (Pratt, 2000). He was also an academic high achiever, constantly turning in some of the best work in the class. Harry was the academic star of the class, equalling the best girls in literacy, and achieving better results than they did in numeracy and science. James was also a very able boy. None of these three central stars had a problem with 'uncool'. On the strength of the sociometric testing and observation, Peter, Harry and James were the role models who set the tone for boys' achievement – in academic work, in sport and music too in Harry's case. This scenario needs to be contrasted with some of Skelton's work, where football is used by working class boys as a status signifier in opposition to academic work. Skelton paints a picture that is more in accord with the orthodox view of a macho, working class, footballing masculinity underpinning a rejection of academic work (see also Pratt and Burn, 2000).

What is to be made of this? One possible explanation is that social class is being overlooked. Peter, Harry and James were all middle class boys, and their primary school, though not without its social difficulties, perhaps contained a critical mass of middle class children. Skelton, on the other hand, describes Benwood Primary School, which was firmly working class. This might suggest that the media debate has focused on gender and ignored social class. This would accord with a general political drift since the time of Bernstein, possibly associated with the school improvement movement, which has characterised a shift in emphasis from such factors as social class towards gender. Academic writing has, to a degree, followed this. However, it must also be stated that Skelton chose Deneway Primary School because it had a more middle class intake, and here too, she found evidence of an association between football and problematic aspects of masculinity.

At Deneway School, Skelton found that male teachers were likely themselves to engage in 'laddish' behaviours with boys in support of football, and that this had the effect of marginalising girls (including the ones who liked football) and boys who did not like football. The situation at Peter's school is complex. I taught Peter, so he had a male teacher, and there were other male teachers in the school. There was no doubt that in running the school rugby team, I encouraged boys' sport. I also taught much physical science, and remember thrilling the class (or was it the boys?) by setting up a live steam railway running round the classroom. However, I also taught music and worked collaboratively with the female head to run the school choir, which was mostly girls. I have already disclosed that in my pastoral relationships with the children, I openly allowed the feminine side of my personality to function. So was I a laddish male teacher and did this account for Peter's success and the absence of a boys' 'uncool' culture? Alternatively, were the boys responding to my openness as a nurturing male with some feminine qualities? Perhaps my gender was just irrelevant.

This is extremely difficult to determine. It provides a salutary reminder of the limitations of analytical categories such as those suggested by Connell (1995), and the fluidity, multiplicity and ultimate uniqueness of gender constructions and relationships. I would caution against the role model argument and suggest that, as the data support, social forces operating amongst the children themselves were more significant than any direct influence I may have had. What can be stated with some confidence is that in my teaching, I displayed both masculine and feminine characteristics, and that the primary school boys more recently questioned clearly did not think the sex of their teacher mattered. There was evidence from these boys, furthermore, of positive responses to a variety of teacher qualities, some of which might be conceptualised as feminine and some masculine. The boys clearly recognised that these qualities could exist in teachers of either sex.

Implications for teaching

We have constantly emphasised the notion of caring about rather than caring for. Jake's story and Peter's both demonstrate this in practice. The positive feature in Jake's story was the way the teacher facilitated whole class participation in a solution and intervened to protect the children from situations that they were unable to manage themselves. There was a genuine care for the whole class to function as a successful social unit, and a positive desire for the children to learn from each other. Jake was not labelled as deviant by virtue of an imagined masculinity in which tenderness and feelings of hurt were absent. At the same time the response to tenderness and hurt was restrained and not smothering. Most importantly, he was not scapegoated but treated as a member of the community.

Case Study

Asa was a particularly difficult Y5 pupil. On one occasion he unscrewed and removed all the wash basin tap handles in the boys' toilets. On another somewhat alarming occasion, he removed all the craft knives from the Design Technology store, with the declared intention of using them as offensive weapons. Conventional behaviour management approaches were all tried with Asa, and none was successful in modifying or containing his acts of disruption.

At the time the school was experiencing a significant amount of bad behaviour during lunch times. Following principles of attachment theory, a 'secure base' unit was established for Y5 during lunch breaks. A classroom was set aside for those pupils who would rather come indoors than join in the usual playground activities. A teacher took overall responsibility for the unit, and a rota of parents was established to staff it. A variety of indoor games, computer activities, reading or talking groups was on offer.

Asa and other troublesome pupils who exhibited negative forms of attention seeking were encouraged to attend. Within a week it emerged that Asa was a talented chess player. Each day he would come in and studiously play chess with another pupil or a staff member. There were no further problem incidents with Asa at breaktimes, and his classroom behaviour improved significantly. Later, a picture of him studiously playing chess appeared in the school brochure as an example of the 'wide range of extra-curricular activities on offer'.

A simple explanation for the change in behaviour provided by attachment theory is that Asa rapidly achieved an attachment state with his chess partner, and this resulted in cessation of the attachment behaviour. This in turn lead to less hostile reactions from other children.

Peter's story was interesting. There can be little doubt that Peter's footballing skill was significant in his popularity. His attitudes, and those of his immediate associates, were influential in determining the attitude of the whole class. Had Peter's football prowess been culturally opposed to the academic aims of schooling, it is possible that a powerful anti-learning culture might have developed which would have been difficult for the teacher to deal with. Peter's friendship group, however, did not constitute a football monoculture, and the teacher was able to relate to the boys through a range of exploratory behaviours that constituted a broad and balanced curriculum. We are not enthusiastic about the current initiatives to involve boys in schooling through football for precisely this reason. Instead, we argue for higher cultural expectations of boys, and for teachers who possess certain polymath qualities: the ability to talk about or coach football as well as the ability to lead singing, inspire poetry or generate enthusiasm for scientific enquiry.

The most important point, however, is the portrayal of the teacher as a manager of the whole class, and as a professional concerned principally with curriculum and learning. Attachment behaviour is not a phenomenon to be confronted head on. Teachers have two significant ways of preventing attachment behaviour through the manipulation of exploratory behaviour. The first is through the management of interactions. Where all else fails, children can be moved from open social situations that are too demanding for them and placed in conditions where they can explore social relationships with a limited number of peers (as with Asa). The ability to engage the interpersonal and emotional intelligences, as well as promote general social development through qualities such as sympathy, empathy and mutual respect is crucial in all other situations. The second way is through the engagement of children in exploratory behaviour. Most children, if given a task they can do, will do it. This can be all that is necessary to stop the attachment behaviour. As far as exploratory behaviour is concerned, we would argue that the recent intense focus on literacy and numeracy targets has been counterproductive whenever it has resulted in the narrowing of learning styles and the insistence that all children conform at all times to a standardised teaching formula. It might still be more appropriate to give a child a task which is motivating and at which he or she can succeed, regardless of targets that have been imposed without reference to local and individual circumstances.

Some individualisation of work is thus necessary, but in overall terms a teacher's relationship is not primarily with individual children but with a class. This requires a unique set of management skills not found in other professions such as social work, where relationships with individuals and families are more significant. In relating to a whole class, teachers must clearly reflect upon how they present themselves as gendered beings. The notion of the androgynous teacher is not a passive one, nor

'Masculine' Pathology	Androgynous Teacher	'Feminine' Pathology
Encourages boys' talk or 'only for the men'.	Talk to whoever you feel comfortable with.	Boys stereotyped as unable to articulate feelings.
Football monoculture or 'geek/anorak' tendency.	Polymath with broad cultural base, able to support children in a variety of activities.	Aversion to all activities considered 'male', especially sport and physical science.
Only interested in superficiality and having a laugh.	Understands that children's relationships likely to flourish when stimulating curriculum draws attention away from personalities.	Over-interested in relationships: tendency to pry.
Hierarchical manager, target and achievement obsessed.	Good team player, able to manage relationships in school as part of collegium.	Uninterested in management.
Competitive control freak Needs to show off to children.	Interested in children, but able to give them the initiative when appropriate.	More interested in staff-room gossip than what children do outside class.
Problems ignored or brushed under carpet.	Knows how to help children resolve their inter-personal difficulties.	Incessant gossip about problems or breach of confidence.
Aversion to any form of intimacy.	Knows strategies to develop independence in children.	Desire to 'mother' children.
Always telling jokes, never serious.	Can switch readily between serious and light hearted with good control	Subscribes to 'boys will be boys' stereotypes or remains aloof.

is it simply a category arrived at through descriptive research studies. There is some danger in classifying qualities by gender. In the summary opposite, we have placed the terms masculine and feminine in quotation marks and use the word pathology to indicate an extreme and unhealthy form of the trait. We risk accusations of steretyping because we believe that the table both summarises the points about attachment behaviour and anticipates what the boys we interviewed say, as reported in the next two chapters.

In the final chapter of this book we look more closely at the associations between gender and the curriculum. We focus particularly upon case studies of music and sport in order to demonstrate the gendered messages children are receiving from the school curriculum, and how boys' and girls' life style choices are significantly influenced as a result. Consistent with the general theme of the book, we find that it is a failure to care about and manage peer culture that leads to gendered behaviour in children. Women teachers are shown to be successful at teaching sport, and men at teaching music.

Summary

- Children who exhibit mainly attachment behaviour are likely to be of low social status and experience the rejection of their peers, which further increases the level of attachment behaviour

- Attachment behaviour is most effectively countered by minimising the situations in which it can occur, and by the provision of exploratory behaviour opportunities in the form of tasks at which the child can succeed and which engage interest

- A broad and balanced curriculum with a variety of opportunities and teaching and learning styles is more likely to promote exploratory behaviour

- Children who exhibit mainly exploratory behaviour are likely to be of higher status and other children may wish to emulate them or receive their approval

- Teachers need to understand children's cultures through an awareness of what goes on at breaktimes and out of school times, appreciating the primacy of peer relationships

- Teachers need to work mainly with the class as a whole in the light of this understanding. Other professionals may be needed to work with some children individually as clients

- Teachers can reflect on their attitudes to the above and are not constrained in doing so by their biological sex

CHAPTER SIX

What boys think about being taught

Introduction – Creating the boy myth

There is plenty of published comment on what boys are like, but almost all of it is from adults interpreting boys' interests back to them. Recently the *Guardian* published an article 'Hitting the Right Button' (19/11/02) which claims 'Boys have a natural affinity for computers'. Do they also have natural rhythm, and love to sing or dance, and are their brains different to girls' brains, rendering them incapable of interest in such activities? It seems that stereotyping the interests of boys is deemed unproblematic. To what degree does it remain similarly unproblematic to state that girls have a natural affinity for caring roles and writing poetry, but are incapable of operating computers?

It is worth looking more closely at what is being said here:

> Lots of boys don't like writing and they're more willing to explore it, trying out different styles and composing longer pieces, using computers. Many boys have difficulty with presentation and neatness and find handwriting a chore.

This begins with 'lots of' – an unspecified number, but clearly more than one or two. We would like to know how many and where from, but we are not told. It implies that boys don't want to write, that they are hesitant to explore the world through imaginative writing. Girls, by implication, clearly enjoy presentation and neatness, and find handwriting a source of delight.

Not merely are boys spoken of as not wanting to engage with writing, they also

> ...massively overestimate their ability and think they can get somewhere without expending any effort. They're also the best barometers of good teaching, and need to know the aims and outcome of the task – if they don't see why they should do it, they won't do it.

What is extraordinary about the above is the confidence with which the author states what boys are like and what their interests are. The article was chosen as typical of what is currently being published about boys in the broadsheet press, the popular press and also by certain academic commentators. The idea that boys overestimate their ability and don't wish to expend effort suggests arrogance and insensitivity, but that is what boys are supposed to be like. As with all similar articles, what is totally absent is the voice of boys themselves. This chapter and the next set out to convey what boys themselves have to say on these issues. We are committed, through our research interests and our values, to telling children's stories. We are mindful of the power of belief and the previous chapter noted the tendency of men to act on beliefs rather than evidence. We are against the creation of damaging beliefs about boys which might eventually become self-fulfilling prophecies.

The research
It is inappropriate to give a lengthy and detailed description of our methodology, but the reader will want some idea of the nature and scope of our evidence and how it was gathered. The work began in the late 1980s/early 1990s with an in-depth MPhil study of a primary school of some 250 children in the South West of England. This involved logging the playground behaviour of all the boys every day for a period of two terms. Fifteen boys at that school were studied in depth. The next significant study from which we draw evidence is an ethnographic study of twenty boys who sing in a church choir, conducted between 1999 and 2001. This study involved detailed diary observation of the boys at choir, as well as two home interviews with each boy and several group focus interviews. A

similarly designed ethnographic study of boys in a scout group is currently in progress and has provided evidence for this book.

During 2001 and 2002, we worked on the project with a total of eight primary schools situated in the South West of England, and covering a range of locations from the inner city to the suburban and rural. The schools were selected to ensure that a broad spread of social class and ethnicity was represented, and particular care was taken to include groups deemed in the literature to be problematic, such as white working class boys and African-Caribbean boys. Boys were observed in lessons and some were interviewed at home. Group and individual interviews were conducted with boys at school using video and photographic material to stimulate discussion and reflection. We have detailed transcripts of interviews with some fifty boys drawn from these various situations. The age range covered was from Y2 to Y6, although the greatest volumes of data are drawn from Y4 and Y6 classes. We also worked with teachers and student teachers who have provided us with triangulated validations and interpretations of our data.

This is not a great number in terms of statistical sampling, but it must be understood that the data are highly detailed and in depth, and that much more sophisticated research instruments than questionnaire surveys have been employed. This is in keeping with other recently published work on gender, and our total sample of schools, homes and youth organisations compares favourably. In this chapter, we report and analyse what boys have said about work, and in the next chapter we do the same for what boys have said about being cared for at school.

Do boys think they are a problem?
According to work we have carried out in primary schools, the short answer to this question is no. We were interested to know whether boys thought that girls did better than boys, and whether having more men teachers would affect this, both in terms of work and behaviour. We were also keen to test out boys' opinions of the oft quoted principle that it's not 'cool' for boys to work hard. Significantly, the boys were at first curious as to why we were interested in their opinions. Once assured of

confidentiality and the possibility that what they said might 'be in a book' they were eager to talk to us. As far as we are able to ascertain, they were candid and frank and we are reasonably confident that they were not simply giving us the 'right answers'.

We carried out the interviews ourselves, two male interviewers. We used the same research instruments but worked separately. Thus we did not visit the same schools, and the boys saw only one or the other of us. We were particularly struck by the degree to which, quite independently, many of our boy interviewees seemed surprised or even shocked by what we put to them.

Many were puzzled and put differences in success in school down to individual difference, i.e. how clever a child is regardless of their gender. Transcription cannot represent voice quality. What was striking when listening to the tapes was the sound of surprise in the boys' voices that anyone could actually think that differences in achievement were directly related to gender. Nor do they think that boys inherently behave more aberrantly than girls. We can see in this extract of an interview with Wayne, Aris and Dean that poor behaviour is the consequence of poor classroom management – as Dean says, 'some teachers don't know what to do.'

Wayne: *Well sort of but it's kind of how we do the work. Some boys don't want to work but mostly they do and sometimes girls are nasty to them.*

JL: mm ...who do you mean, them?

Wayne: *Oh yeah like other girls.*

JL: What about boys?

Wayne: *No they don't do that*

JL: So what about work then?

Wayne: *Well there's some boys that mess about an' that but so does some girls. I don't think girls are better. It all depends on how good you are at the work... so if you're doing maths an' you know how to do it you are better aren't you but if it's like hard then it's hard for everybody.*

Aris: *Maybe 'cos there's some clever kids an' they could be girls but some are boys in this school. Well mmm like last year three boys went to a clever school.*

JL: What's a clever school?

Aris: *You know you pass this hard exam and then you can go but not if you don't pass.*

JL: I see, but have you heard that girls are better at exams?

Aris: *No not in this school but in some other places they could be.*

Dean: *Yeah I've heard it, but it's not true 'cos if it was, then girls would always be best and they're not ... sometimes boys get good marks.*

JL: I've heard some people say boys don't like school they mess about an that...

Dean: *Well some do but you know like some teachers don't know what to do when kids mess about so it's not their fault is it? Then they don't do the work so they don't do good.*

JL: Is that boys?

Dean: *No ...it's some but could be anybody.*

Stewart and Adam, in the next interview, are Y6 boys who both attend a difficult inner city school which has several male teachers on the staff, including an evidently well liked Y6 teacher. The overall results of the school reflect its difficult circumstances. In terms of boy/girl balance, they are broadly in line with the national average, so there is no evidence that the presence of male teachers has increased boys' scores. Stewart is a boy who has done well in his SATs, in spite of the 'disadvantage' of a high proportion of working class children who might, according to conventional wisdom, be expected to deride effort by boys. He was asked whether this had been a problem. '*In this school they don't really care about it. I think in most schools they say if you're brainy you're a geek, but in this school it doesn't matter because a lot of kids are good at work. Most of the kids are good. We get some level 5s. I got three level 5s.*'

His classmate Adam, of average attainment, seems to agree with Wayne, Aris and Dean at the previous school.

MA: So do you think girls do better than boys? *Boys are more into fights. I'd say they're (boys) better at hobbies and sports.*

MA: But what about actual school work? *I wouldn't say in this school. Most of the boys in my class are smarter than the girls.*

The notion that most of the boys are smarter than the girls was an interesting one, and it could reflect the claim made by the writer quoted in our introduction that boys 'massively over-estimate their ability'. It would be unfair, however, to portray Stewart in such general terms, as he came across in interview and class observations as a pleasant and modest individual. Some girls were spoken to during the course of our interviews, and Chantel is an African-Caribbean girl in the same class as Stewart and Adam.

MA: So who do you think does better at school?

Chantel: *Boys.*

MA: Even the ones interested in football?

Chantel: *I don't know really. Even the ones interested in football. They're a lot brainier.*

MA: So who does best in SATs? *Boys. Say there's about 30 kids. 21 boys will do it and girls won't. They're a bit low like me. I got all 4s except three 2s. There's this boy called Nick. He gets 5s.*

MA: Is it fair? *Yeah, because he knows a bit more than me. I think it's fair. He deserves the level he got 'cos he works hard. He takes his time and I don't.*

The conversation with Chantel revealed an ethnic minority girl apparently locked into a cycle of poor self-esteem and low ex-pectations. She had some ideal ambition to become a midwife, but had evidently already accepted that this might be beyond her and that it would be the brainy boys that went on to achieve. As we have said, the results of this school were similar to national patterns, but the attitudes revealed here should caution any who wish to introduce remedial programmes to boost boys' achievement. It is unlikely, from our knowledge of the teacher, that the attitudes were the result of a pro-boy discourse, even though that teacher was male. Unfortunately, we have no sustained evidence of daily classroom talk over a period that would allow us to make a judgement about this.

We found little difference between the attitudes of the Y6 boys at these two schools and the Y4 boys interviewed at this third school. The boys in the next interview had not experienced a male teacher, although there was a male postgraduate trainee working in their class. As with the Y6 boys, these boys did not recognise the underachievement of boys as a problem. They also expressed a universal rejection of the 'boys don't work because it's not cool' sentiment. These are 1:1 interviews conducted in a corner of the classroom while the other children work. The second and third extracts in particular reveal surprise and strong feelings.

MA: Another thing I sometimes hear is that boys think it's not cool to work hard at school.

Carlo: *I'm not that sort of person. I like doing neat work because I'm proud of my work. I take quite a long time to do it.*

Later, to Mark, MA: I've heard that some people are saying girls do better than boys at school.

Mark: *They do? Please tell me who said that!*

MA: Well...some people to do with the government...

Mark: *Tony Blair! Phah! Big deal!*

MA: So it's not right?

Mark: *No. I reckon it's just cruel.*

MA: OK. Well, I've also heard it said that people say boys think it's not cool to work hard at school.

Mark (He pulls a big, indignant frown): *Why? Please can you tell me?*

MA: Well, I'm hoping you can tell me!

Mark: *If it was somebody I knew, I'd have a word with them* (said menacingly).

Mark's classmate, Joey, in a later interview validated this attitude.

MA: Well, some people are saying that boys aren't working very well at school.

Joey (pulling an extremely expressive face): *AS IF!*

MA: Some are saying that boys think it's not cool to work hard at school. *No! You have to work because you have to learn and if you don't learn when you grow up you'll have no job.*

MA: OK, well, the government, you know who they are? (*nods*) are saying these boys might do better if there were more men. *Why are they saying that? I'd work for a man or a woman. I'd just get on.*

The classes in which these interviews had taken place had previously been shown a video by their class teacher which showed short extracts of various men and women teachers at work, and references to the video were made in the interview in order to draw out children's experience of teaching style. The children had been told that 'the university wants to know how you like to be taught' and had been asked to identify which video teachers they would most like for their next year's teacher (in the case of Y4) or their form tutor at secondary school (in the case of Y6). Gender was specifically not mentioned. The children were simply asked to comment on the teaching styles. The table opposite summarises their responses.

Statistical analysis reveals a large standard deviation, which confirms the degree to which pupil responses were idiosyncratic and centred upon personal preferences for teaching style rather than any trend towards gender identification and preference. The only significant preference was for Female 2, who received the highest ratings of all four teachers, and was a clear preference amongst the Y6 pupils for their Y7 tutor. This was the judgement of both boys and girls. The qualitative data confirm that neither the gender nor the race of this teacher (she

Table I

Pupil Ratings of Video Teaching Episodes

	Boys				Girls				All		
	Sch 1	Sch 2	Sch 3	Sch 4	Sch 1	Sch 2	Sch 3	Sch 4	Boys	Girls	All
M 1	2.2	1.5	2.6	3.4	3.0	2.0	2.7	2.1	2.5	2.5	2.5
F 1	3.4	2.4	1.8	2.5	3.8	3.3	3.0	3.1	2.2	3.2	2.7
M 2	3.4	2.9		2.7	3.0	3.1		2.2	2.9	2.7	2.8
F 2	3.7	3.4		3.8	4.4	3.6		4.3	3.6	4.1	3.8

is black) were explicitly taken into account. It was her confident, enthusiastic teaching and visible rapport with the pupils that appealed to both boys and girls. The following comment was made by Marcus, a Y6 boy in Stewart's class (see above). It is typical but also interesting in the way it likens the female teacher to a known male teacher:

Marcus: *That one. She taught it how it is. She was fun. She made the work fun like Mr K. does. I want more teachers like that. They teach what they're supposed to teach and make it fun too.*

The following conversation took place with Mitch, a white working class Y6 boy in another challenging inner city school. Mitch had earlier been observed to defy his woman teacher.

MA: OK, which of all the teachers would you prefer?

Mitch: *Mrs A* (said with considerable assurance).

MA: Why?

Mitch: *Because she don't make us work too hard or make us write too fast.*

This might support the proposition that Mitch, whether he liked it or not, might work better with a strict male teacher. However, the conversation continued about the performance of Male 1, whom Mitch had watched with me on video. The video included reaction shots of the children's faces.

Mitch: *They're scared of him.*

MA: Would you be?

Mitch: *Yeah.*

MA: Why?

Mitch: *He's big.*

MA: Are you a bit scared of big men then?

M: *Yes.*

MA: So what about moving to secondary school. Will there be big scary men there?

Mitch: *Yes* (he looks genuinely apprehensive/worried).

MA: Well. Do you think the other man teacher was scary enough to make the children work?

Mitch: *He's not really scary. They'll behave because they'll really like him.*

MA: Do men have to be big and scary to be tough, proper men?

Mitch: *No, not really.*

This interview took place with Mitch when the rest of the class had gone to practise their assembly, Mitch having been excluded for his behaviour. He had been quietly working on a maths task when I approached him with the request that we watch the video again together. The situation was one of a male inter-viewer working with an outwardly 'laddish' boy who was willing to disclose to a sympathetic man his private fears and feelings of insecurity. It is at this point that the intertwining of the issues of work and caring become apparent. Many interpretations could be placed upon the observations of and interview with Mitch. He had been seriously defiant of his woman teacher, yet liked her better when offered the possibility of a man. His defiant behaviour might thus be the result of personality and the way a particular incident was handled rather than gender. His fear of 'big men' is particularly notable, given that he attended an inner city boys' club, where the main activity appeared to be boxing, led by a man who clearly had his respect.

What sorts of teacher will boys work for?
The dilemma provided by Mitch thus takes us almost seam-lessly into the question of role models. Is it true that boys will work and behave better when they have a male teacher as a role model? The evidence reviewed in the previous section already suggests perhaps not. When the question was put directly to the boys, the answer we received was as clear and unambiguous as the answer we had received to the work is 'uncool' question. Again, no – it appears that boys would not work and behave better for men. In summarising the responses of all the boys we spoke to, we can state with some confidence that boys will work

for any teacher who is good, regardless of their gender. Indeed, we have distilled this useful definition of a good teacher from the boys in all eight of the schools visited. It is not dissimilar to other statements made by children about what makes a good teacher:

- Reasonably strict but fair

- Not grumpy

- Explains things well

- Helps you with your work

- Makes the work fun

- Has a sense of humour.

The next few exchanges are taken from a Y6 class in another school, also situated in a predominantly working class district. In this school the children had the experience of a male teacher (the deputy head) and a female PG student on final practice. After discussion of the video scenes used to elicit responses revealed no preference for male or female teachers, this conversation continued about the actual teaching experienced.

MA: You have Mr J and Miss C teaching you this term. Does it matter which one you have?

Sean: *Not really.*

MA: So which would you choose if you could?

Sean: *Miss C.*

MA: Oh...why?

Sean: *'Cos I think she's a good teacher and she wants to be a teacher and she'll learn more about how to be a teacher.*

MA: But will you learn as much from her?

Sean: *I don't know really. They're both good teachers.*

The choice of Miss C does not actually appear to be explained here in terms of teaching quality. However, another pupil in the class volunteered the following without being asked.

Matt: *We have a lady and a man teacher here.*

MA: So which would you rather have? *Miss C.*

MA: Why's that?

Sean: *Because Mr J's more likely to go mental.*

The perceived likelihood of male volatility emerged as a negative theme, and is noted here by a Y6 boy in another school:

Ed: *Women are calmer, and they don't have a go at you that much.*

MA: So when you go to secondary school?

Ed: *A woman.* (said confidently and emphatically).

MA: Why?

Ed: *I can't say,* (thinks)... *I'd rather have a woman tutor. They'd be calmer.*

The idea that men would be stricter or more disciplinarian was upheld by eight unsolicited comments about male strictness as opposed to two about female strictness. It was recognised, however, that men could be gentle and kind, whilst women could be strict. Men were simply more likely to be strict. Male volatility and strictness, however, were not generally regarded as virtues in terms of work and achievement. Darren, a Y6 boy interviewed at home with a friend in Y5 commented: '*Men are too strict. They shout at you loads.*' The boys were asked, in relation to a teacher they knew, whether this might nevertheless be a good thing in terms of achievement.

MA: So if he's strict, would you work better or worse?

Darren: *Worse...definitely.*

MA: Why?

Darren: *Dunno.*

MA: Are you scared of him?

Darren: *No.*

Lee: '*He puts me off. We like the teacher we normally have and we miss her.*'

Darren and Lee both attend a relatively small rural school and are clearly comfortable with the woman teacher they have known for two years. Familiarity would seem important here. Later in the interview, it was put to Darren that he might be a bit 'soft' for preferring his familiar woman teacher to men who might be stricter. This triggered a switch from serious to fantasy mode.

MA: Darren...from what you've said, you seem to prefer lady teachers who aren't strict or big ... might this be a bit wimpish?

Darren: *Wimp? No! Anyone shouts at me and I'll kick 'em.*

All but one of the other comments about strictness equated excessive strictness with lower achievement, including one comment where a woman teacher in the video sequence was disliked for being 'really strict' and compared unfavourably with a man perceived to be '*really encouraging ... She isn't.*'

The one Y6 boy who thought male strictness a good thing was in the class with the female trainee. He seemed concerned by the fact that '*...when Miss C is teaching, they think they can muck about.*' Perhaps on the basis of this experience, this boy preferred shouting to kindness? '*Shouting. 'Cos they've gotta learn their lesson.*' MA: 'So you don't mind if your teachers shout?' '*Not really.*' This episode is an interesting commentary on the notion of male role models. Shouting does not feature on the list of qualities of a good teacher, and is clearly disliked by the majority of boys. Yet it seems to be a behaviour more likely to be modelled by males, and which in this case undermines the teaching of the female trainee.

Kindness as a virtue occurred five other times in unsolicited comments, three times for women, and twice for men. It was again recognised that either gender could be kind. With the exception of the Y6 pupil above, kindness was linked to higher achievement, as in the case of this Y4 boy commenting at home on a National Literacy Strategy video showing a male teacher at work in KS1. Jonathan: '*He was kind to all the children. He told them what they did wrong so they'd learn.*' These extracts again confirm that gender is not an issue. Men can be kind and women can be unhelpfully strict. Men can be unhelpfully strict and women can be kind.

The demand for 'appropriate role models' in the popular discourse is nevertheless unceasing. It applies to men for boys and ethic minority teachers for ethnic minority pupils. The views of black MP Dianne Abbot, who claims that black male teachers are needed for black boys and blames white women teachers for the poor performance of black boys, were put directly to Jemal, a Y6 African-Caribbean boy in our study. He disagreed with Abbot's analysis.

MA: Do you know what a role model is?

Jemal: *Yes.*

MA: Have you got one?

Jemal: *No.*

MA: Why not?

J: *I just want to live my life and not copy anyone else.*

MA: Are there any bad role models?

Jemal: *No.*

MA: So what about racism, have you experienced it?

Jemal: *Not by teachers.*

MA: So by whom?

Jemal: *Some kids in this school. I don't mind so long as I'm learning.*

Jemal was not particularly enthused when told that there was a black MP who thought there should be more black, male teachers. *She might be right.*

The question was also taken up with Jinny, an African-Caribbean Y6 girl recently over from the USA. Here it seems that both gender and race are fundamentally irrelevant to the qualities of a good teacher.

MA: Does it matter to you whether it's a male or female teacher?

Jinny: *No.*

MA: So does it matter whether your teacher is black or white?

Jinny: *No. They should be a good teacher.*

MA: But are there enough black teachers?

Jinny: *No.*

MA: Why do you think that?

Jinny: *I don't see enough of them. There should be more.*

Jinny supports the boys' view that the first priority must be for good teachers, and that these can be male or female, black or white. Her suggestion that there should be more black teachers because she 'doesn't see enough of them' would seem to resonate with the principle suggested in Chapter 1, that the make up of the teaching force should reflect the make up of society. Jinny seems wise here in recognising there should be more black teachers in general, but that any attempt to compensate for supposed role modelling problems by matching gender to gender and ethnicity to ethnicity is as futile as it is irrational.

An interview with Sacha, an African-Caribbean Y6 girl in another school confirms both the inadvisability of ignoring girls in the problem-with-boys discourse, and the inadvisability of paying too much attention to assertions made by MPs. Sacha expressed clear distaste for the notion that black teachers might be needed as role models for black pupils: MA: 'So should there be black teachers for black kids?' Sacha: *'No, 'cos I'm black. There was a black teacher in Y4. She didn't like me. She wanted to be the only black person. She'd say 'not good enough' and 'you've messed it up' an' she'd get on better with a white person even though she was black herself.'* None of the ethnic minority pupils spoken to expressed a confident desire for ethnic minority role models.

None of our conversations with boys resulted in any of the popular discourse issues being raised by the boys, and we had taken particular care not to exclude specific mention of gender or role modelling from our interview schedules. The topics were only pursued when they were raised by the children themselves, or when it seemed natural to do so as part of the conversation. In this last episode, a scenario was put to some boys in a group interview.

> Your family has to move to Manchester and so you leave behind all friends at primary school and you don't know anyone in Manchester at all. Once you have moved house your Mum takes you to your new school to meet the Headteacher. The Headteacher welcomes you and says that there are two classes you can go into and one is taught by a lady teacher and one by a man and you can choose which class you want to join.

Even bearing in mind all that has been said about the issues, we were surprised at the nature of the responses. William gave the question a great deal of thought, then said: *Well it's a bit hard... mmm...'cos I won't know anybody if I chose here I'd go with my friends in this school but I couldn't. I think I'd have to wait to know who was the good teacher. Maybe I could ask, but how would they know?...What you want is the best teacher really.*

JL: What do you mean the best teacher?

William: *Oh you know. The one that helps you the most so that you do well.*

JL: What about your secondary school then?

William: *I'm going to Uphigh School... my mum says it's the best and the kids work hard and don't mess about there. They got good teachers you see.*

The other pupils made similar statements that they couldn't choose because they had no information of the quality of the two teachers. As in all the interviews reported in this chapter, gender was not significant. The boys wanted the good teacher who, as John said, *'helps you to understand and to do your work.'*

What does all this mean? Are boys not a problem?
There is little that is liked more by the media than a public disagreement between leading scientists. Indeed, the best copy is usually when one maverick scientist, who may or may not turn

out to be an Einstein, says something that the scientific esta-blishment disagrees with. We do not wish to cast ourselves in the role of such mavericks. In theorising upon the findings re-ported above, we are mindful of the academic literature that provides evidence in support of the fact that boys, in general, may be problematic. We have already suggested that the bulk of this literature is based upon work with adolescent boys, and we would repeat our view that it is unwise to assume that it applies to younger boys. Nevertheless, the mere fact that primary school age boys do not see themselves as problematic (accord-ing to our work) could itself be part of what may become a problem later, if it is not already a problem by the end of primary schooling.

The tradition of work undertaken in secondary schools has created an established discourse of laddishness, the masculine ideal of 'effortless achievement' and the 'uncool' nature of working at school. This is a well established tradition, perhaps with roots in Willis's seminal study of working class masculinity (Willis, 1977) and endorsed by significant writing during the 1990s, such as Sainsbury and Jackson (1996) or Haywood and Mac an Ghaill (1996). Noble and Bradford (2000) simply regard the argument that boys positively promote an anti-swot culture as irrefutable (p 15). The particular line of questioning ('Well ... some people to do with the government...') that was used to elicit the responses from the boys we interviewed was inspired by what has passed into history is an infamous speech made by former government minister Stephen Byers (Byers, 1998).

In the speech, Byers attributed boys' underachievement to a cult of 'laddishness'. Francis (2000) has carried out work with secondary aged pupils based directly on this speech, and found that 67% of secondary (mainly Y10 and Y11) pupils agreed over-all with Byers's proposition that the laddish behaviour of boys is impeding their learning. Of this figure, 70% were girls and 64% boys. Clearly, this is problematic. The most straightforward ex-planation is an essentialist biological one related to puberty – an explanation which, while contestable, would not be in con-flict with sociological theories of masculinities and social con-structivist explanations based on changing discourses of adolescence. However, the issue is surely not this straight-forward. In particular, acceptance of these kinds of explanation would overlook:

- The fact that if boys' laddish behaviour is disrupting lessons and inhibiting the effectiveness of teachers, then girls should also be disadvantaged (Warrington and Younger, 2000, p493) Laddishness is thus a weak explanation of boys' relative underachievement

- That as Francis (*op cit*) acknowledges, girls also engage in significant anti-teacher/school behaviours, and there are, in effect, feminine forms of laddishness whereby girls reap the 'patriarchal dividend' of complicity in boys' masculinity. Connolly (1998) furthermore reminds us that such be-haviour by girls is consistently more negatively evaluated than for boys. Reay's study of primary children found that laddish behaviour by girls resulted in teachers' use of terms such as 'real bitch' and 'little cow' (Reay 2001).

- The possibility that increased laddishness amongst older boys is actually partially the result of increased exposure to male teachers is a disturbing one for which some evidence is accumulating (Skelton, 2001). This possibility would be concordant with our own findings amongst primary school boys, and undermine the popular argument that more male role models are needed to improve boys' behaviour and achievement

- That although Foster, Kimmel and Skelton (2001) acknow-ledge that boys are well represented amongst the highest as well as lowest achievers, there may nevertheless be a ten-dency to create, within the post-Willis discourse, a focus on the values, attitudes and behaviours of white working class boys. This may reflect a bias in researchers' interests more than an objective summary of the total situation of boys

Worryingly, there are also questions to be asked about the degree to which any of the research has unravelled all the pos-sible strands. There are parallels to be drawn from the school effectiveness literature which demonstrates the extreme difficulty of isolating the effects of any one teacher. Although Muijs and Reynolds (2001a) argue for a focus on effective teachers in preference to effective schools, sophisticated multi-level modelling by Creemers and Reezigt (1996) found that teacher difference accounted for only 3% of variance in pupil performance. Given the relative infrequency with which primary school children are taught by men, the reliably measurable effect of a male teacher role model in a classroom must be almost infinitely small. If there is to be any serious manipulation of boys' performance relative to girls, it seems that it must be undertaken at a whole school level, inevitably by women teaching boys in the main. We just cannot say what effect a male teacher has in the long term.

We would not claim that our results are more valid, reliable or objective than those of Francis. However, there are questions for researchers to ask themselves about the different consequences of male and female interviewers working with boys and men, girls and women. The principle, derived from particle physics, that we cannot be objectively certain because the observer creates the behaviour of what is being observed needs to be remembered. In the case of Francis's work, a female interviewer hands power to boys by presenting them with the Byers construction of lads as antiheroes. This could be interpreted equally in terms of a feminised school culture unable to cope with them, or a masculine culture which, on principles of adolescent rebellion, must be resisted. Either way, the sociological discourse of hegemonic masculinity is given a further airing.

The evidence of our younger boys could be considered more reliable simply because of the factor of childish innocence. These boys have not yet begun their teenage bids for independence and are possibly less likely to play devious games with the researcher than older boys. Even here, however, there is an issue of age differential. Boys might tell a different story to someone who is closer to them in age than they do to researchers whose own children are grown up. This possibility shifts the focus onto caring and relationships, which is taken up in the next chapter.

CHAPTER SEVEN

What boys think about being cared for

Introduction: Questioning the orthodoxy of laddishness

The dominant discourse in academic writing, as well as popular versions and 'how to teach boys' type publications, is the sociological perspective of hegemonic masculinity that looks to R.W. Connell. This perspective is itself used by a significant number of serious writers to challenge the essentialist position (i.e. boys' brains are different) that has been popularised by writers such as Steven Biddulph. A significant critique of the essentialist position appears in Gilbert and Gilbert (1998). Fundamentally, we do not take issue with much of what has been written in the sociological writing about masculinity, but we do feel it has been overemphasised. In this chapter, we stress alternative perspectives that are more in line with our theoretical foundations in attachment theory, and our argument that too much that is written about adolescent boys is assumed, uncritically, to apply to younger boys.

There is, for example, an account of boys' behaviour that is offered by the self-worth protection theory espoused by Covington (2000). Jackson (2002a), draws upon it to remind us of an alternative discourse that is hidden. Boys here are posited not as strong and macho, but as only appearing so because of inner insecurity, the fear of failure and a secret fear of feminine superiority. This fear, paradoxically, may be fuelled by the discourses of hegemonic masculinity. Another alternative account of 'boyishness' is offered by Phillips (1993), who takes issue with Walkerdine (1981). Walkerdine interprets the behaviour of four year old boys as positioning themselves powerfully in relation to their nursery teacher through sexist, violent and oppressive language. Phillips, however, finds this hard to believe and prefers the interpretation that 'they felt lost in this great big world with no Mummy figure to look after them' (p 209). Interestingly, she continues by describing a gender difference in which girls monitor the behaviour of their peers and pull the unruly back into line. The boy who is 'neither cute nor charismatic, but is miserable or demanding' will not have the attention of a peer group seeking to modify his behaviour. 'He will simply be left alone' (p 210).

Citing these authors illustrates the point that the mediation and interpretation of boys' behaviour by writers and researchers is a highly subjective process that is particularly susceptible to the influences of authors' world views and value systems. There is little evidence to justify some of the confident assertions made about boys. The discourses offered by Jackson and Phillips however are valid, and certainly complement the work on attachment behaviour drawn on for this book. The term 'complementary' is preferable to 'alternative' when describing these discourses in relation to the dominant sociological discourse of hegemonic masculinity.

Francis's (1999, 2000) work with adolescent boys seems to reach a different conclusion to findings about primary age boys. There has to be an explanation for the different stories the boys tell her. That the boys interviewed are of different ages is perhaps the most significant factor, but there may be differences related to the gender of the interviewer. Significantly, Francis identifies the reasons put forward by her Y10/Y11 boys to explain their laddishness:

- innate differences between gender

- greater maturity of girls

- pressures from, or the need to impress, friends

- wishing to appear hard or macho

- wishing to impress girls

- female keenness and willingness to work

- parental influences on boys

- socio-cultural expectations of boys

- more distractions for boys

- women's liberation

- girls worried more about job prospects/boys take future for granted

- boys more competitive (Francis, 1999)

This is an interesting collection of apologetics for laddishness, but notably absent is any recognition that laddish behaviour might be the result of inner insecurity and fear of the feminine. In the remainder of this chapter, we present and analyse evidence that most primary school boys, including the 'hard' working class ones, have a 'soft' inner self that is easily hurt. This inner hurt can be the source of behaviour judged bad or laddish by teachers or others. The conclusion, drawn by some popular writers, that boys are somehow 'emotionally illiterate' and less capable than girls of discussing inner feelings and emotions is shown to be unjustified. Instead, we show that primary school boys are still heavily dependent upon their mothers, sensitive to their peers and appreciative of any teacher who controls the class well. Prevention or resolution of peer conflict would seem to be the most important caring attribute teachers can have here. Most boys did not look to teachers as 'mother figures' and tended to recoil from the idea.

A window into boys' feelings

We showed boys a large colour photograph of an obviously distressed boy, aged about nine, sitting hunched on the floor, wiping a tear from his eye, and invited them to speculate on what might have happened and how the boy might be feeling. We then encouraged them to say what ought to happen next in the story. Through this, we progressed to hearing stories about their own feelings, and their views about pastoral care. Once again we received a straightforward and unambiguous answer, summarised by Carlton, a Y6 boy of mixed heritage: *Because teachers aren't family and there's no way they could really do what families do.*

Carlton is expressing a widely held a view. Boys do have intimate feelings and are fully capable of expressing them. Teachers, however, are not people with whom you share intimate feelings. This is confirmed by Ben, a Y6 pupil at another school, in an interview with a friend. The two boys were adamant that they would not talk to *any* teacher. It is difficult to square these judgements with the fact that even these two were generally well disposed towards school.

JL: You wouldn't talk to a man or a lady teacher?

Ben: *No 'cos it's not for them ... it's about me so I'd tell my mum.*

JL: Would you never talk to a teacher?

Ben: *Yeah* (somewhat emphatically) *about your work and that and if it was bullying or if it was someone else they might need help.*

Although both boys state they wouldn't talk to a teacher, they later modified this. There is a sense in their replies that hurt feelings are private not public, hence talking within the family is appropriate. They talk to teachers about school things, 'your work and that'.

Interestingly, they say they might tell a teacher about how they perceived the feelings and needs of another child. This concern for the feelings of others, and the fact that the boys talk about it, confounds the stereotype of tough boys who can't share or express feelings. Significantly also, it supports our view that teachers should care *about* rather than *for*. The role they see for teachers is as managers who sort out the kinds of problem that occur specifically at school. This is clear in a response from one of the youngest boys we spoke to. Graham, a Y1 boy, was interviewed at home. He is clear that the upset boy problem is one for peers and not teachers.

Graham: *He should be helped by someone ...one of his friends.*

MA: Suppose he didn't have a friend to help him, who else might?

Graham: *One of someone ... one of his friend's friends.*

MA: What about grown-ups?

Graham: *No, I don't think so. Only if they're kind.*

There was little evidence here, then, of the expectation that teachers are there to care *for* you and give you a get better hug.

This is echoed by Stephen, a Y4 boy, also interviewed at home.

Stephen: *The person should apologise or you should go and tell a teacher.*

MA: Would he? (the boy in the picture).

Stephen: *Probably, if he felt like it.*

MA: Would you? *I don't think I'd have a chance. My friend Sam sorts everything out. He's a good friend at school. Sam would sort it.*

Stephen and Sam, then, would appear to be two boys who share feelings and help each other. Their feelings, however, are not shared with teachers, and it is possible that the authors of books who claim that boys do not talk about feelings mistakenly attribute it to emotional inarticulacy. However, the expectation that teachers *should* care *about* is present in the interview with Stephen. Many of the boys interviewed at school tended to define a pragmatic interventionist role for teachers. Although for most, friends were clearly the most significant 'hands on' carers, the presence of adult authority in the background was reassuring.

Marcus, a Y4 boy interviewed at school told a similar story to Peter and Stephen. Marcus: *'My other friend Jamie, he came over and helped. I feel safer when there's teachers looking after me, but I like friends around too, but not too many.'* The expectation of teachers emerging seems to be not that they do the caring but that they intervene authoritatively when friends are unable to resolve the issue. The 'tell a teacher' message seems to have struck home with Andrew. *For him to tell someone and they'll sort it out for him.* MA: 'Who would sort it?' Andrew: *Teachers if it's in school or if it's at home his mum and dad.* 'Sorting it out', however, does seem to be a management (caring about) role rather than a motherly (caring for) role.

This is apparent in this next extract with Richard, which also indicates a new theme: the possibility that a man might be better at this management role.

Richard: *He'd be more strict to the person that done it. So it would work better.*

MA: So did you feel that bad?

Richard: *and he kicked me as well.*

MA: Was this at school? What did you do?

Richard: *I told the teacher. The teacher told him off. We shook hands and carried on.*

Here, Richard is speculating on the teachers in the video extract described in the previous chapter. 'Male 1' teacher in particular is perceived as potentially competent at 'sorting it out'. This perception of male teachers occurred independently in other schools, and is evident in two extracts where the boys were commenting on the video sequences of male and female teachers at work.

Steven: *'Cos ... (thinks)... no, it doesn't matter. He'd be more grown up.*

MA: What would more grown up be?

Steven: *Let them ... just sit them down and calm down.*

On another occasion, with Tim:

MA: So, if you felt bad, you would also go to him?

Tim: *Yeah.*

MA: What would he do?

Tim: *He'd say, don't worry, I'll have a word with the boy, don't you worry, you'll be all right. Be a brave lad.*

MA: Would you like that then?

Tim: *Yeah. He'd say get up, don't worry. If you were picked on he would have a word with them.* <u>*She*</u> *wouldn't.*

Generally, the evidence suggests that in principle boys are happy with teachers of either gender acting in this management, caring *about* role. However, unlike the cognitive, 'subject delivery' question, we did find tendencies to judge by gender. As the above extracts confirm, there is a tendency to perceive males as more competent at being in control and 'sorting it out'. The caring appreciated by Tim and Steven seems matter of fact and pragmatic rather than mother substitute. Such pragmatic qualities were more commonly attributed to males at school, whilst mothers at home were more likely to be recognised as the most desired intimate confidants. In the next extract, we see some suspicion of women teachers who might pry too much into personal matters, as opposed to men who would talk less but be more fun.

Four Y6 boys in a group interview, after some deliberation, opted for a male teacher. They were unhappy, though, about not knowing what kind of teacher (other than gender) they were choosing. The reasons for choice are intriguing.

Alan: *Well if I* <u>*had*</u> *to, (choose) ... a man 'cos you'd get games but women can be scientists as well.*

JL: What?

Alan: *Women and men are scientists aren't they?*

Darren: *Yeah I think then a man because a lady teacher would talk to you and want to know too much.*

Peter: *Oh a man, they are more fun, jokes and that and they might understand more.*

Colin: *A man 'cos they're strict and could sort problems out with other kids like Mrs B does in our school.*

This is significant. Although they made a gender choice, each of these boys was hesitant. Being made to choose seems to have resulted in some use of stereotyping. Alan appears in his comment on scientists to have an emerging understanding of gender stereotyping. Darren both stereotypes women as more talkative and prying, and confirms Carlton's views: it is not for teachers to pry into personal relationships.

Colin, however, exhibits a classic confusion. He believes in the stereotype that a man would be a tough disciplinarian. But he knows from his experience that women are equally capable of being disciplinarian: – a *man* would sort it out, just as *Mrs B* does! There is clearly a tension in many of these interviews between the tendencies to stereotype and a tendency to generalise on the basis of experience. The limited experience some boys had of male teachers must be an issue here, although we were unable to identify clear differences between those boys who had men teachers and those who did not.

Do boys have preferences about carers?

We found degrees of confusion and ambiguity with regard to caring that we did not find with regard to subject delivery. The evidence indicates that boys prefer teachers who do not fuss, do not pry into personal things and who take a pragmatic approach to sorting out any difficulties between children. This might well also be the preference of girls, although we did not ask. It seems unlikely that girls would expect their teachers to mother them any more than boys do. Although we found no tendencies to stereotype or express gender preference in relation to subject delivery, there *was* some tendency for boys to stereotype men teachers as more capable than women of a pragmatic approach to caring. As was particularly the case of Colin and Mrs B, there was some confusion and imaginative thinking surrounding this issue. Men teachers were expected to be more fun or tell jokes.

We did find some evidence of feelings of greater comfort from female care. In the next extracts, Billy, A Y4 boy, is able to articulate this.

Billy: *Female teachers make me feel more better because I'm used to females looking after me.*

MA: OK, but can men look after children?

Billy: *Yeah. But I reckon ladies are better. Men really don't do exactly the same stuff as females.*

MA: So what's this 'female stuff' you mentioned?

Billy: *I don't know. They just have something about them that makes me feel happier and safer.*

This was not a unique response. James, a Y6 boy in another school, offered this as a reflective afterthought when the interview had ended: '*I actually think the woman teachers are more motherly. Not offensively, just kind and understanding, but I wouldn't mind a man.*' MA: 'Oh ... so can a man be kind?' '*Yeah, if they want to.*'

It was difficult to separate responses based on clear experience from responses based on speculation in response to our questioning. The view that men would have more insight into boys' problems because they had been boys was fairly common '*Because men understand you better*' (Y6 sch 2). '*Men understand more because they've been boys.*' (Y4 sch 3) '*I don't know. Probably because I'm a boy myself. They* (women teachers) *might not understand.*' (Y6 sch 1). There is thus a slight tension between perceptions of women as more comforting and men as more understanding of boys, but it is unlikely that either feeling is based on sustained personal experience. There was no correlation between boys expressing such an opinion and experience of being taught by men.

That some degree of speculation or fantasy is involved is confirmed by Jamie, a Y4 boy.

MA: Did you know that some of the government people are thinking boys might work better for men teachers?

Jamie: *Yeah.*

MA: Would you work better?

MA: *Yeah.*

MA: Why? *'Cos boys can understand us boys, and girls can understand girls.*

However, Jamie seems confused by his own proposition when confronted with his actual experience. MA: 'Do you think Mr H understood you more than Mrs W?' Jamie: '*I think ... (pause) ... I don't know.*' (The expression on his face suggests probably not.) The use of the term 'boy' to refer to a male teacher is interesting, and we encountered it several times in different schools. It is possible that boys may perceive things very differently to adults. The role model argument might be an adult view that ignores boys' perceptions.

Chris in Y4 seems to be saying that men teachers might be desired as big, same sex friends, rather than perceived as particularly effective with boys.

MA: Well, do you like males?

Chris: *Females are more friendlier for looking after you. No offence, but males would be better for a friend, and sometimes older ones like Mr H.*

Andrew, another Y4 boy makes it even clearer. Andrew: '*Not really. You know, some boys probably reckon that males understand your work better. Lewis, who's left this school, said 'I want a boy teacher, like a cool one', so he doesn't have to work.*' 'Understand your work better' appears here to mean expect less in terms of work. Yet in the previous chapter we heard of Mitch's stated preference for his female teacher who 'don't make us work too hard or make us write too fast'. There would seem to be some interchangeability of gender of teachers perceived as easygoing.

Sean, a white, high attaining Y6 boy, summarises the imagined relationship, and speculates on the feelings of girls: '*Girls are really close to female teachers. Boys don't like teachers at all, but would be closer to males because they relate to them*'. This important proposition connects with the notion that girls are advantaged by having teachers of the same sex. We tested this idea out with some girls. Charlene is a Y6 African-Caribbean girl, interviewed with her white friend Jasmine.

MA: The boys said to me that men would understand them better because they've been boys. I'm wondering if that's fair because there are more lady teachers for the girls.

Charlene: *No way! Because it was a long, LONG time ago. Not the same problems. It was a different time.*

Clearly then, age difference is far more significant than gender. Adult teachers of either gender are hopelessly out of touch with pupils' personal concerns. We encountered this attitude elsewhere, and it resonates with the quantitative finding (summarised shortly) that peers are preferred to any adult outside the family as confidants.

The conversation with Charlene and Jasmine turned to the question of race.

MA: So what about racism? Would black teachers understand black pupils better?

Charlene: *No, because racism happens on both sides.*

MA: So does it make any difference to you?

J: *No.* MA (to J): Do you trust white teachers to be fair?

Jasmine: *Miss A has absolutely no sense of rhythm* (both girls mimic actions all out of time).

MA: But is she fair about racism? *Yes. If a white person does something bad, she tells them off.*

Racial fairness is defined here as telling off black and white children an equal number of times. This is interesting but hardly surprising.

The response to the specific question about black boys having white women teachers was significant for two reasons. First there seems to be a recognition by the two girls that African-Caribbean boys start school well and their performance declines more rapidly than their white counterparts. This is supported by statistical data. Second, however, the African-

Caribbean girl reveals her personal experience of this process. Not much is heard about this, pointing yet again to the dangers of girls' invisibility in the problem-with-boys discourse.

MA: So what about black boys with white teachers?

Jasmine: *Yeah, in Old Oak Hill it is* (racist).

Charlene: *I have a (black) friend. When he came here he was all breezy, but he* < words lost, gist was that his performance and interest in school rapidly deteriorated >

Jasmine: *That happened to me too in Y3 and 4.*

Jemal, a Y6 African-Caribbean boy, featured in the previous chapter, was dismissive of Dianne Abbott's notion that black boys need black male teachers as role models. This is consistent with the idea that teachers are too old to be confidants or role models. Where gender is concerned, the matter probably ends there, but on the race issue, strong cultural forces obtain. Abdul, a Y6 Bangladeshi boy, was forthright about how he would be cared for if he felt like the boy in the picture. It was not a matter for teachers. It would be his two big brothers who would comfort him, not his teacher, and not his mother.

Abdul: *They care for me.*

I: Do they care more than your mum?

Abdul: *Yeah.*

I: How do you know?

Abdul: *'Cos when I got beat up, one of my brothers came in and helped me.*

Interestingly, Abdul had been observed earlier in the day putting his arm round another boy and offering what appeared to be a genuinely tender act of caring.

It seems naïve to promote the notion that ethnic minority teachers are needed because they can be caring role models for pupils of similar ethnicity. We find the work of Carrington and Skelton on role models and teacher recruitment interesting here. The Pakistani female student below is describing to

Carrington and Skelton her feelings of rejection in relation to her desire to be a role model. It was not white working class boys that particularly upset her, but Asian girls:

> when I was rejected by the females I found that very difficult ... I offered myself and my support to them ... I think I'm probably so much older than them anyway that I've lost touch with the way they think these days. I think generally the Asian girls are quite difficult to deal with and I couldn't handle them at all. (Carrington and Skelton, forthcoming, p 16.)

Our evidence indicates that age bars any teacher from being the supercharged role model that some commentators seem to yearn for. Adults outside the family do not equate with parents (mothers in particular) as carers or role models, regardless of gender. This suggests a passive rejection of teachers as role models. It simply does not occur to boys that their male teachers might be role models unless they are asked. However, when ethnicity is also taken into account, rejection can become active and fuelled by cultural norms and this appears, perhaps paradoxically, most likely in relation to ethnicity. This is not to say that boys reject teachers. Our research shows that this is far from the case. Teachers are respected by primary school boys of any ethnicity when they have the ability to *teach*. It is quite clear that boys will judge by this criterion and any teacher must prove him/herself to the boys through teaching ability, not through motherliness, similar ethnicity, or the pretence of being an heroic role model.

Summarising and categorising the responses
We asked the boys to indicate by means of a numerical analysis who they would most probably turn to for emotional support. The results are shown in Table 1 below. The numbers are means of a scale of 1-10 in which 1 represented definitely wouldn't and 10 definitely would. Gender is clearly a less significant factor than social role. It can be seen that in each case, social roles come paired by gender in the rankings, with little difference accounted for by gender. There is in each pairing a marginal preference for male over female except in the case of parents, where mothers are preferred to fathers.

Table I
Boys' Reported Preference for Emotional Support
(39 boys across 7 schools)

1. Mother	8.8
2. Father	8.2
3. Friend same age	7.6
4. Older boy	6.4
5. Older girl	5.9
5. Nobody	5.9
5. Male teacher	5.9
8. Female teacher	5.7
9. Brother	4.5
10. Sister	4.3
11. Male youth leader	2.9
12. Female youth leader	2.0

The next most significant pattern is that adult family members are preferred to non-family members, although this is not the case for siblings. Sibling rivalry, as well as pragmatic considerations articulated by some respondents such as their brother being only a baby, would account for this. Of non-family members, there is a clear and unambiguous preference for same age friends, with older boys and then older girls being the next most likely to be turned to. Non-family adults are relatively unlikely to be approached, although teachers fare significantly better than youth leaders. On the basis of our evidence, familiarity or *frequency of contact* accounts for this. Children of primary age seem unlikely to confide in, for example, a cub leader they meet only weekly.

The preference for peers and older children over non-family adults is significant in relation to the attachment behaviour reported in Chapter 4. These new findings confirm the earlier findings that peers, not teachers, are the principal attachment figures at school. Attitudes, values and behaviour patterns are more likely to be influenced by peers than teachers, further undermining the role model argument. On issues such as drugs or sex education, boys might be more responsive to older boys than to adults, and this is beginning to be recognised. The Channel Four sex education series *Living and Growing*, for example, shows a significant shift towards presentation by children rather than the teacher-like adult 'experts' of earlier series.

The data in this chapter contradicts the orthodoxy promoted by some writers that boys are emotionally inarticulate. All our informants indicated that they thought it important to talk to someone about 'how you felt when you're not happy'. We see that they do talk with a friend of the same age, perhaps with an older boy or girl, and with parents. We found no evidence of the supposed tough boy laddish refusal to engage with emotional difficulties. We *have* found evidence that the social role of the person talked to is the most significant variable, and that gender is much less significant. Teachers and writers who see things from teacher perspectives may be misled into viewing boys as emotionally inarticulate because they are the people boys generally talk to about their feelings.

This chapter began with revealing comments from two Y6 boys in different schools, talking independently to different interviewers. Carlton said: 'teachers aren't family and there's no way they could really do what families do'. Ben said: 'No, 'cos it's not for them. It's about me so I'd tell my mum.' These comments typify the evidence we have reviewed that supports the idea that primary teaching is not substitute mothering. Ben went on to state that he would talk to teachers if it was about work or to draw the teacher's attention to someone else's need for help. Ben's pragmatism and straightforward response sums up much of what we have said. Of course you talk to teachers about your work – that's what teachers are there for, to teach. No, you don't talk to teachers about your feelings. Feelings are personal, and you share personal feelings with close friends and parents. Significantly, Ben remarks that he would tell a teacher about another child who might be in some emotional difficulty, most probably because of bullying. Our interpretation is that boys do care *for* each other, and that they expect teachers to care *about*, to manage relationships at school and to teach well.

Two case studies

Case Study I

'Help! What do we do with Damien? He says you're the only teacher that's ever understood him!'

These words were spoken by the head of Y7 at Damien's comprehensive school to his former Y6 teacher. Damien's year head had telephoned his Y6 teacher one evening out of the blue, in an apparent act of desperation.

Damien had been described by the head of KS1 at his primary school as the 'naughtiest boy in the school'. He had certainly figured prominently in the ethnographic study of boys' social relationships at that school. His reputation for defiance of the dinner ladies and running amok at lunchtimes was legendary. His challenging classroom behaviour throughout KS2 ensured that his status as one of the top 'hard lads' was assured. It was only in Y6 that Damien began to calm down, become more sociable and apply himself to work.

During an interview with his Y6 teacher, Damien slowly dissolved into tears and confessed that his 'hard' behaviour was because he was scared that people would make fun of his poor reading ability. He was frightened about going up to 'big school'.

Question for reflection
Damien's confession and improved behaviour was due to a successful relationship with a male teacher. It was achieved through that teacher's belief that Damien's behaviour was motivated by self-worth protection – that behind the 'hard' exterior, there is usually a hurt and frightened inner child.

• Could it equally have been achieved by a female teacher?

• Were expectations of Damien based upon a popular boy stereotype?

• Was the attitude of the head of KS1 helpful?

These case studies illustrate how stereotypes of what boys are supposed to like affect the work of schools. Damien went through a whole primary school career in which it was assumed that his macho behaviour was inevitable, and that any attempt to appeal to a more gentle or caring side of his nature would be pointless. Yet the principle of self-worth protection would seem to describe his case. Engaging earlier with Damien's concealed sense of inadequacy might have lead to a different outcome. This possibility is particularly pertinent at a time when schools are forced to comply with a competitive regime that, whilst giving political and marketing impressions of rising standards,

Case Study II

'We make all our supply teachers cry, you won't last long.'

These words were spoken to Samantha, a postgraduate trainee, by ten year old Ross, affirming that Downlow Avenue School is not an easy place for a trainee to complete her final teaching practice. Samantha, however, had a previous background in social work and was committed to developing a relationship with the challenging working class boys through mutual respect and trust. She admitted to making the mistake of thinking them more grown up than they were, and was amazed at how well they responded to what she had imagined to be the overly childish rewards of good work stickers. They pleaded to be given the butterfly stickers she was handing out – until the male deputy head scorned these as girlie.

The incident with Adrian took place after he might already have been upset by overhearing some remarks made by the teaching assistant. Apparently Samantha's methods were 'daft college ideas' – too soft for the likes of him. He had enjoyed some science work earlier in the day, but had sullenly refused to write it up. Samantha judged that the time was right to push him over the matter. She judged wrong. He stormed out of the classroom, kicking over tables and chairs in his way. Later, he reappeared with his mother, who forced him to apologise. He burst into tears. Samantha commented in interview on the difficulties he subsequently faced in re-establishing his 'lead stallion role'. Apparently the other boys kept going 'boo hoo' every time he spoke.

Question for reflection
Adrian appeared to experience a conflict between 'soft' and 'hard' methods of relationship building. The school's expectation seemed based upon a 'hard' model. Butterfly stickers were derided by the male deputy head as girlie, even though the boys liked them. The teaching assistant seemed to have low expectations of boys' ability to build caring relationships. In spite of the school's macho expectations, Adrian's emotional relationship with his mother seemed to provide evidence that he might not be the miniature 'hard man' implied by the attitudes in the class room.

- What role did stereotyped expectations of boys play in this incident?

- Does this incident confirm the evidence that mothers continue to be the most significant emotional others for Y6 boys?

- What would be the best way forward to develop relationships between female staff and the boys in this school?

also generates high stakes failures. That there may be a relationship between this and the perception of a problem with boys merits investigation. Examining the association between the results of schools that care about their boys through an emphasis on building relationships, and the results of schools that seem to expect boys to be macho would be equally useful.

This is hardly an issue of teacher gender. It would be possible to interpret case study one in gender terms, since it was a caring, understanding male teacher who positioned himself against the stereotyped expectations of boys. But in case study two, it was a female trainee teacher who had begun to achieve some success in challenging macho stereotypes and generating a classroom atmosphere built upon higher expectations of boys' ability to care and form relationships. She had, however, to work against the influence of a senior male colleague who promoted a macho attitude, and a female teaching assistant who seemed complicit in this. There is some suggestion of the weaker positioning of the female teacher in a male school management culture. What is surely called for is an androgynous culture, in which the qualities of caring about, as we have defined them, are dominant.

CHAPTER EIGHT

Teachers and mothers

In recent years national and public agencies have commented unfavourably on the way in which boys do or do not benefit from primary schooling. Comments on the achievement gap are a feature of the Annual Reports of the Chief Inspector for Schools. Most recently Atkinson and Wilson (2003) report that the performance gap between boys and girls at GCSE is widening and argue that government policy should therefore focus on boys' achievement. Teachers have been subject to a plethora of advice on what they should do to combat the 'problem of boys'. We look briefly at examples of advice given to teachers in recent years in England and in Australia that indicates that the 'boy' question pertains all over the English speaking world.

The TTA funded project directed by Gary Wilson sets out a programme of action for primary school teachers which arises from their reflection on their own practice and what they believe about boys. The programme of action was drawn up by teachers who had conducted action research in their own classrooms and then shared the results thus creating a pool of good practice. The project highlighted the need to work to develop high self-esteem, to have behaviour policies to combat 'bullying and other unacceptable elements of 'boy culture''. It is also claimed that boys learn in a different manner from girls, so need to be given work in short achievable chunks and to have the aims and objectives made clear. The recommendations made by the Select Committee on Education and Training of the

Australian Parliament House of Representatives are similar to those in England: that the achievement of boys be monitored at national, state and school level and that teachers combat boy culture and raise boys' academic self-esteem principally by recognising boys' learning styles. Particular mention is made of the 'fact' that 'verbal linguistic learning styles are usually preferred by girls as girls tend to talk more and have larger vocabularies than boys'. And the report asserts that 'boys respond better to teachers who are attuned to boys' sense of justice and fairness and who are consistent in their application of rules.' In Australia as in England it is boys from 'lower socio-economic groups that are failing to achieve'.

We discussed working with boys with two experienced women teachers in the light of the recommendations made to teachers in England and Australia. What were their beliefs and values about the education of boys? And was their view of boys part of their general professional identity? We conducted an ongoing professional conversation, held over three visits to school.

Both teachers work in multi-ethnic schools in areas of social and economic disadvantage. Dee is a KS1 teacher with responsibility for ICT development in the school alongside her responsibilities as a class teacher and senior team member of the school. Dee has engaged in a wide variety of CPD and recently gained an MA in education that explored the use of ICT to enhance the literacy skills of disadvantaged KS1 pupils. Maureen is the deputy head teacher of an inner city primary school; this is her second deputy headship, in a school much larger than her first. She has considerable management responsibilities in the school and is currently concerned with improving the quality of teaching and learning, particularly in Key Stage 2.

Both teachers were successful and highly respected professionals and both took responsibility for improving the quality of teaching and learning in their schools. They had been consistently responsive to professional development and had critically accepted recent central government initiatives, particularly the literacy and numeracy strategies and, in Dee's case,

ICT. Both teachers were alert to an achievement gap between boys and girls, although Maureen pointed out that the three most successful children in the present Year 6 were boys.

Dee, Key Stage 1

When asked whether there were consistent differences between boys and girls, Dee was somewhat ambivalent. '*Sometimes there is a difference in the way children learn but it's difficult to link that directly to what is being said in the media at present.*' She believed that individual differences were at least as significant as gender. '*In this class there are a lot of children with specific needs*'. This is hardly surprising in the context in which she works. Dee's school has a high proportion of pupils in poverty, which itself is highly correlated to special educational needs. In addition a significant number of Dee's pupils are acquiring English as an additional/alternative language. So it is natural for her to focus attention on individual children's needs rather than gender or other group differences.

One of the constants in the commentary on boys is that they are more demanding than girls and are likely to take the lion's share of the class teacher's time. Dee's response to this was was very complex. '*Yes some of them do demand more attention but for different things. I can think of three boys in this class who – yeah are disruptive like if it requires reading. Yeah it's the special needs that get the attention but it can be difficult to separate the two. Well for instance the boys are trying to play when they shouldn't or not concentrating on the task but it can happen with girls. I've got one or two so it's not just a boy thing.*' She thought that demands for attention were related to the kind of activities they were engaged in, and their specific needs. '*Well, one boy can get on quite well in number work but needs lots of help in literacy where he goes into a world of his own.*' She continues, '*He knows he's not as good at his literacy and he knows his targets for writing then he sort of goes off anyway but doesn't become disruptive and stop other children from working.*' It is the fact that this pupil and some others '*know they are not so good*' that affects their learning and behaviour. Dee's initial responses demonstrate her deep knowledge of the individual personalities of her pupils, how they work, and how easy or difficult they found learning tasks. This might indicate that gender differences were insignificant for Dee. But this is not so.

The conversation turned to the question of disruption: who are the disrupters and what are the causes. This has been a major theme of the debate about boys and girls and primary schools and the particular 'problem' of disruptive African-Caribbean boys. We expected Dee to have an incisive view. It was that boys tended to be more disruptive than girls but that demanding behaviour was due above all to personal and learning needs. In her view it was the age of the children that was significant. She had no doubt that African-Caribbean boys were likely to become truculent when they were older as they responded to the pressures of a racist society but at KS1 they were not yet reacting in this way, she said, elaborating: *'Disruption is really sort of a matter of access. Well in order to access the curriculum, the learning, they need to be able to do certain things and some of them find it hard. When they can't get into the activities they become disruptive.'* While the problem of disruption is difficult if not impossible to overcome, the school has made important structural changes which reduce disruptive behaviour. This restructuring has provided extra support to all pupils but especially those in greatest need. *'What we are doing is responding to learning needs not behaviour but they all know about behaviour policy you know they can get rewards and that.'* Dee also noted that this reorganisation had reduced the disruption problem of the two girls as mentioned above.

It is common for teachers to be advised to ignore problem behaviours on the principle that by not rewarding them they will be extinguished. Does the structure, by acknowledging their behaviour, reward it with attention and so compound the problem? Dee thought long and hard before she said, *'Well, I don't really respond to their behaviour, it's the learning needs and that goes for them all.'* Teachers should always respond a professional manner. Good teaching leads to good learning and it's the school's and teachers' job to promote good teaching that leads to effective learning.

The Australian Report, the TTA and the work reported by Gary Wilson all argue that boys need male role models and that they have some difficulty relating to women and girls. For Key Stage 1 we must take into account the pupils' social and emotional development. It is relevant that a significant number of children in Dee's class have poor friendship skills. Unsurprisingly Dee wants to ensure that children behave well towards each other whatever their ethnicity, race or gender, '*I always encourage them to behave positively to each other, children bring with them different things, their own way of behaving and we challenge that, they need to behave positively towards their peers regardless of where they are coming from.*' The shift from the first person singular to the first person plural pronoun marks how individual teachers in a collegiate school operate in line with how the school as a whole interacts with pupils individually and at group level.

We put to Dee that as well as being a classroom teacher she was an authority figure across the school because of her seniority. Her response was incisive: '*No they don't they respect me as a teacher and I respect them as individuals and I have never had any negative words or anything. ... I know of some conflict that's happened with other teachers but that's what happens sometimes.*' When we probed again whether children and particularly boys responded to women differently as authority figures Dee insisted 'No I don't know of any sexist responses like that from the children.' About Dianne Abbott's claim that African-Caribbean boys respond better to black teachers, Dee said that maybe '*some of the Muslim boys had a little difficulty relating to women but that might be a cultural thing, I can't really say ... it's not verbal, it's more attitude*'. Dee had not spoken to her male Key Stage 1 colleague about how children reacted to him but it did not seem any different.

The school has recently reviewed their pupils' progress and achievement within the National Curriculum. What teachers were asked to do was to rank their pupils by subject using a variety of assessment instruments. '*We were looking at assessing numeracy and the number of boys who were top in their class were more than girls and that was from Year 2 to Year 6.'* We queried whether the results would be the same for literacy. *'Well it would be interesting but it probably wouldn't be the same.'* We were interested to know whether literacy materials were more girl friendly than boy friendly, as argued in much of the literature. Dee's response was *'I try to choose things that are not gender based, things that would appeal to anyone. I mean I suppose it depends on what you're doing like you're doing something on feelings and I know a lot of people would say that's not a boy thing. When we are talking about it boys are equally able to talk and to express feelings as girls. Although I remember one boy who just wouldn't or couldn't, but it's just one you know.'* What is being said about numeracy would offer some support to the idea of boy and girl friendly subjects flagged up in much of the literature. Recently Dee has established an after school ICT club and has noted slightly more boys than girls attended it but she is ambivalent about whether this is evidence of the boys' predilections to IT. *'IT hasn't been opened to Key Stage 2 yet and anyway boys may be staying for reasons other than the attraction of IT.'*

Maureen, Key Stage 2

Maureen is a dynamic deputy head with a burning desire to ensure that children receive justice and are enabled to learn to the best of their ability. She has a brief for reviewing the performance and achievement of all the pupils in the school and is much interested in gender, ethnic and cultural differences. Her work in her previous school and this one leads her to maintain a critical professional interest in advice offered to schools and teachers on the education of boys. She acknowledges problem of underachievement and that this affects boys somewhat more than girls but she was a adamant that this wasn't the whole picture. *'Actually the three best pupils are boys in Year 6 all of them are going to Lowtherbridge School* (a prestigious HMC school in the city) – *they've passed the entrance exam.'* In this case she identified the problem not as boys' underachievement but as the failure of teachers to recognise their intelligence and talents and be concerned to act to ensure that pupils can and do make proper progress.

I: 'Do you think that boys are really very different from girls in how they learn?' Maureen's response was thoughtful and detailed. *'Well some maybe – many are more kinaesthetic, they like action and speed a bit more than a lot of girls. Often they want to work quicker and they like it to be faster and pacier but that's not all boys though.'* She believes the girls to be *'much more relationship based'*. While this sounds like a formula for teaching boys, it became clear that Maureen was really talking about matching pedagogy to how they learnt, a desire to build on the learning processes they were best at. This thinking is connected to a school policy, not just for boys but for all pupils. In part it draws on Maureen's experience in her previous school.

We were interested in Maureen's views on the use of mentors and role models from outside the school, particularly black and ethnic minority role models and mentors. *'I think it's good to have male role models in schools for boys ... some don't have much of that at home because of circumstances ... but it's what you do with them, outsiders are good but what you really need is high quality teaching.'* She described how in her previous school they had sought to bring in adults who were successful. About a black solicitor who came into the school on a weekly basis and read with the pupils she observed: *'Fine, but what about them knowing how he came to be a solicitor – they can't get that by reading to him or with him.'*

Maureen's previous school was in an area of even greater social disadvantage an area of the city with a reputation for criminality, in particular drug dealing and prostitution. What the school wanted to do in its role modelling mentoring pro-gramme was expose the children to adults who were successful at work. *'OK a lawyer's great but lots of people are important and have done well ... so we got a local taxi driver to talk about his job and how he liked it and it made money and that ... this business of role modelling and mentoring isn't just about people with high class jobs but showing pupils how ordinary people from their community are really significant and important.'* Simplistic role modelling is not enough, in Maureen's view. Her account suggests that the notion of male mentoring and role modelling is somewhat crude and that a more thoughtful and subtle approach is needed.

Boys and girls need to be able to express and explore their aspirations but this requires more than asking what they would like to be when they grow up. '*Well there seemed to be something about girls – they seemed to have a more mature understanding and they want to be things like teachers and TV presenters ...* (laughs) *but it's really about self esteem.*' She thinks children need realistic information about occupations and career possibilities, hence the introduction of local workers of all kinds. '*We wanted to show particularly the boys that all jobs are valuable and useful, the taxi driver and the council worker ... it was important because of the prevalence in the area of 'high earners' who dealt drugs or were petty criminals.*' I: 'So a good mentoring role modelling programme needs to ask the children who they are and how do they feel?' '*If they don't think about how they feel about themselves how can they have proper aspirations?*'

'*Boys do need good role models but in school what you really need is high quality teaching.*' The crucial question is what constitutes high quality teaching. Pace and fast action had already been identified as significant for boys, but not for them exclusively. The ability to recognise talent even when it is disguised by unacceptable behaviour traits, as with the three boys she talked about, is important. A powerful whole school mechanism for flagging not just poor performance but also high potential is monitoring. Careful use is made of all available mechanisms and resources. Currently the school is focusing on the improvement of performance at Key Stage 2, using standard and formative assessment to attempt to help make a better match between teaching and learning. In doing this the school is following central government recommendations on targeting and extending its resources to make full a use of 'booster groups' for both boys and girls.

Maximum use is made of QCA Year 5 tests and pupils who fall into level 3 a/b bands become a focus of attention and constitute booster groups. On this form of organisation Maureen commented *'This has been interesting because actually the boys are achieving more.'* Booster groups were not always easy to implement. Initially boys questioned their organisation and wanted to reject them, whereas girls were much more accepting. What the boys demanded was an explanation both of the organisation and why they were being placed in the groups. Boys seem more likely to be suspicious of a scheme that could be interpreted as placing them in lower ability groups. They asked for and were given careful explanations, which related the grouping to their needs in ways that *'they can understand'*.

Careful monitoring and reorganisation can and do contribute to the creation of high quality teaching but is not sufficient. Although Maureen perceives boys as demanding more active and 'quicker' learning, she constantly stresses quality of teaching rather than favouring a separate pedagogy for boys and girls. *'High quality teaching is when the actual teaching matches where the children are ... you have to match where the children are and I think it's when the curriculum is culturally and linguistically of benefit to the children. And where the children are engaged and responding and where the children are happy and there is an emphasis on the teaching of values and it's a really positive environment and they know they aren't going to be spoken to sarcastically and they have proper guidelines ... no it's not to do with men and women, it's just good teaching.'* Maureen's idea about pedagogy implicitly critiques the National Curriculum. She values a pedagogy that prioritises children and the relationships that teachers have with them rather than knowledge specified by the National Curriculum. Maureen has visited schools in Washington DC to explore questions of underachievement. *'You know they teach values separately there ... I was at my other school and we did a lot of 'Can Do' stuff but I started to do that. We need a core set of values that need to be taught and they are about valuing people and should be in everything, marking and displays, speech.'*

Maureen's critique of the current curriculum and pedagogy in primary schools goes much further. She is convinced that boys need pacier teaching and that they learn best when they can *'see where they are going'*. In an ideal teaching world this would not come about through a prescribed National Curriculum or specified content in, for instance the Literacy Hour. *'No I think the Literacy Hour has done a lot but some of what is used isn't very good for boys.'* Like a number of commentators, Maureen thinks more attention needs to be given to the selection of texts, *'there's a bit too much fiction you know – boys like some factual stuff that interests them ... but then we should find that out for all kids shouldn't we?'* The way it enables teachers to *'keep going at a fast pace...you doing it quickly then knowing you've done it'* is another positive benefit for boys of the Literacy Hour. She thinks the main curriculum ignores the teaching of values and relationships other than superficially. And she believes that we need to spend more time on expressive subjects such as art and dance. *'We had a dance week and everybody was involved – there was total involvement, boys and girls ... they learnt dance from different cultures and were able to see how important these artists were.'*

The school had also been part of a project through which the children communicated their lives through the medium of photography to other children on an all white, socially disadvantaged peripheral estate. We attended the final presentations and exhibitions of this work. The quality and sophistication bore out Maureen's contention that an expressive curriculum enabled the children to deal with issues of self-esteem and feelings. It was also obvious that Maureen was right to say that the children in her school experienced enormously rich home cultures.

A major theme of the 'boys crisis' is disruption and poor behaviour. Maureen's current school and her previous one are in locations where behaviour would be expected to be a problem. We were interested to know whether this was Maureen's perception. She said it was. She compared the kind and level of disruptive behaviour with what she had experienced in a shire county school where she had worked. There unacceptable behaviour was *'a lot of low level stuff – sort of attention seeking, shouting out, which can bring things to a stop. There is some serious stuff but that's kids who have very severe problems.'* She sees disruptive behaviour of this kind as caused by what she describes as a learning deficit and that this is as a result of the mismatch between the curriculum and the pupils and the failure to involve the pupils in what *'really interests them'*.

Girls too can be disruptive. It is difficult to have control of the curriculum itself, but Maureen's school tries to make more use of 'pacey' and kinaesthetic learning and to keep a major focus on pupils' self-esteem and self-worth. Maureen's energetic espousal of a 'Can Do' programme was obvious in her interaction with one of the three of her academic stars in Year 6. David came into her office and she immediately told him how well he had done and introduced him to us as an important person in the school. *'Oh what am going to do when you go to secondary school I won't have anyone to write poems for me ... Do you know David has written a novel and poems and a soap opera?'* Although this interchange focused on a high flyer it is typical of the way Maureen interacts with the pupils, constantly reflecting back to them an image of their worth and value.

Mothers

Although we are certain that the home lives of boys must be important in the formation of their attitudes to school and society, we could discover little about the 'ordinary' life of boys in 'ordinary families'. We decided to approach three mothers, selected on the grounds of having only sons, two of them from professional middle class backgrounds and one working class mother who lives in a small village. Laura, middle class, has three sons aged six, eight and twelve. Mary, who is working class, also has three sons, aged seven, nine and twelve and Eileen, a middle class professional, two sons aged ten and twelve. Eileen works fulltime outside the home as a primary teacher; the other two mothers work part-time outside the home.

We were interested in what they knew about the question of boys and achievement in schools. Laura had gathered information from friends, *'I know quite a lot I've got from friends who have children further up ... they don't seem to be very worried but they know boys who don't really work.*' Mary had a slightly different perspective, 'Yeah well I know some of the older boys round here who don't seem to do much in school ... they aren't a nuisance or anything they just don't work and I don't want mine getting in with them.' As might be expected of a teacher, Eileen was well aware of the current debate.

When we asked whether they thought boys behaved differently from girls the initial response of all of them was to laugh. '*How do I know? I've only got boys*' (Laura). When we persevered, they said they thought boys wanted to be more active – that they enjoyed physical activities but not at the expense of things like reading or playing indoor games. All said that their children were very keen on computer games but that they knew from friends that girls were equally keen. What all of them deplored was the lack of large open play spaces in schools. Laura: '*The school playground is so small that the children can't really run around.*' Eileen made a similar comment about the lack of space but regarded this as a problem for girls too.

All these parents had boys who were heavily involved with out of school activities. Mary explained that her boys went to the scouts but put that down to the fact that her husband had been an enthusiastic scout when he was young and had very much encouraged them to join. '*He likes taking them ... I think he'd like to join himself.*' Laura's boys were also involved and her husband had been a scout leader. We had to ask the football question. '*Well, they're all sort of interested but only Jamie – you know my twelve year old – plays in a team ... I think they feel they have to be ... maybe it will be different when they get older*' (Eileen). The general picture we had was of boys doing a variety of activities being influenced into them as much by parental enthusiasm as by identifying the activities as boy friendly.

How did the boys enjoy or respond to school and schoolwork? '*They don't sort of react the same – you see they are all different ... now Jamie who's the footballer is always reading but I worry a bit about Martin. He's a good reader but doesn't do it unless I say how about reading a book*' (Eileen). Laura noted how different her boys are, '*Danny, he likes exams. He used to say, Oh it's SATs tomorrow, like it was a treat and he's really looking forward to exams in his secondary school, but Andrew, what he likes is making things. He'll spend hours with models and he likes cooking ... well cakes anyway.'* Rather like the teachers, the mothers didn't identify anything as particularly boy friendly but talked instead about their children's personalities. How aware did they think their children were of what was currently said about boys? They replied that the boys knew something, depending on age, about differences in achievement between boys and girls but that it did not worry them.

To what extent did their sons express their feelings? *'Which one?'* said Mary, *'of course the young one still tells me a lot but as for my twelve year old I have to drag information out of him ... but he still tells if he's upset ... I think that's an age thing, not a boy thing.'* On the whole these mothers were puzzled that we should ask the question – except Eileen who said *'of course they are supposed to be little toughies aren't they? – but they aren't. That's just people looking for excuses.'* From her professional standpoint she believes that the issue of feelings and emotions is used as an excuse for poor pupil-teacher relationships. Mary thought much the the same, *'I know a boy who's older than mine. He hates school but I think they don't want to get on with him, because chats away at home.'*

Interestingly, what both our teachers say about teaching boys is mostly about good teaching. They believe that boys are able to express feelings and form relationships but that sometimes schools impede them from doing so. The mothers share these views, unsurprisingly. While Maureen does have a view that boys need to be taught in slightly different ways at certain times, she does not deny that such teaching would also benefit girls. Mothers and teachers represented here are somewhat puzzled by the furore about boys being radically different from girls, but there is a hint in their responses of wondering whether boys are being stereotyped and consequently treated unfairly.

CHAPTER NINE

Towards an androgynous curriculum

Introduction

This book has drawn on evidence that challenges the prevailing view that there is a problem with boys. And our own findings do not suggest that the shortage of male teachers to act as role models is nearly as significant as some would claim. Our extensive conversations with, and observations of, primary school boys did not reveal boys as needing or deserving of special treatment. This sets us apart from those who would like to see boys treated as a special case and, by implication, privileged over girls. On the contrary, we have seen boys from normal, everyday backgrounds who want to do well at school, who recognise and applaud good teaching, who dislike classroom disruption and expect teachers to control it, and who do not subscribe to the 'work is uncool' idea. Above all, boys do not see teacher gender as an issue. The argument for male role models does not withstand scrutiny.

Our findings make it clear that primary school teaching is not substitute mothering. We have portrayed the caring side of primary teaching as a managerial function of caring about organisation, curriculum quality and the oversight of children's relationships. The successful caring primary teacher participates in the creation and implementation of policies to prevent bullying, for example. He or she does not confuse his or her role with that of parenting. We have also demonstrated the importance of peer relationships and the need to work with them and and strive to develop them so that they are a positive force in school.

This is not to say that the present situation is satisfactory. There are indeed not enough male primary teachers. We would like to see more – but not because boys need male role models. The teaching force should reflect a satisfactory model of society, for boys *and* girls. A staff of women teachers ruled by a male head teacher is most emphatically not a satisfactory model. Neither do we deny that girls outperform boys in high stakes testing such as SATs or GCSEs. But testing regimes and the priorities of educational discourse have changed more than the relative performance of boys and girls. We might become concerned about boys' performance if ever females began significantly to outnumber males in positions of achievement, prestige and power in society.

Tidying the loose ends in this final chapter, our argument takes a slightly different turn. Our critique is based not upon the 'poor-boys' discourse but on what we perceive to be the narrowness of the primary school curriculum. Newly qualified teachers are arguably better able to teach the basic skills of literacy and numeracy but this enhanced skill has been acquired largely at the expense of other areas of the curriculum. High on the casualty list of neglected subjects come sport and music. Interestingly, organised football for boys is thriving outside school. Music has suffered badly. In primary schools, it is poorly taught and school choirs are often dominated by girls. Outside school, only a minority of boys participate in music. This is not a crisis of feminisation. On the contrary, we read the situation as masculinised. A narrow curriculum driven by competitive targets is the product of hegemonic masculinity. So is a monoculture of football which offers few opportunities for boys to make music or participate in other arts.

Questioning the stereotypes of football and singing

There is a view that boys are into sport and girls into bookish pursuits. The writer we quoted in the opening chapter stereotyped boys as being 'naturally interested in ICT'. Such ideas lie behind some of the remedies to the problem-with-boys offered by politicians. The problem is to be solved, apparently, by curriculum materials sponsored by premier division football clubs and the recruitment of footballing male role models as teachers. Our evidence does not support such patronising interventions and, furthermore, suggests that girls' needs and interests are being neglected. We have shown that girls are as critical as boys of the inadequacy of primary school sport and the incessant obsession with literacy targets.

Table I below was produced from the recollections of all the Y6 children (n=147) in two of our partnership schools. The children were first asked to reflect on the subjects they had enjoyed during their primary schooling, and then on a range of generic activities abstracted from the subjects. The latter are shown below. The numbers are means derived from a scales of 1-5 where 1 = hate and 5 = like.

Table I
Activities Abstracted From Subjects

Boys		Girls		All	
1. Sport	4.9	1. Computer	4.3	Sport	4.6
2. Computer	4.8	2. Painting	4.2	Computer	4.5
3. Painting	4.2	3. Sport	4.1	Painting	4.2
4. Experiments	4.1	4. Experiments	3.3	Experiments	3.7
5. Writing stories	2.6	5. Writing stories	3.0	Writing stories	2.8
6. Reading	2.5	6. Reading	2.1	Reading	2.3
7. Writing facts	2.2	7. Writing facts	1.9	Writing facts	2.0

It is clear that there are no significant gender differences. The same three activities feature in the top three choices of both girls and boys. Several of the girls we spoke to said that there are insufficient opportunities for sport in primary schools. We found little evidence, in terms of children's actual preferences, to support the notion that boys (as opposed to all children) suffer from sport deprivation, whilst girls are happier with a passive, literacy dominated curriculum. One pupil speaks for several who volunteered an explanation for dislike of the Literacy Hour: *'because all you do is sit on the carpet and read with the teacher, then sit down and write and it's boring.'* This might be thought of as a typical boy comment but it was made by a girl, and is representative of similar sentiments expressed by girls as often as boys.

Also notable is the fact that using the computer, often stereotypically a 'boy thing' was the most popular activity with girls. Girls included sport in their top three whilst boys included painting. Despite supposedly being a 'problem', boys were generally a little more positive in their recollections of school than girls, averaging 3.6 as against girls' 3.3. We do not, therefore, see solutions to the problem-with-boys lying in the direction of a supposedly 'boy friendly' curriculum dominated by football and football club sponsored literacy and numeracy texts.

On the contrary, we caution against any rushed and ill-judged manipulation of the curriculum to make it more boy friendly. The possibility, of discriminating against girls (and the many boys who are not motivated by what are imagined to be 'boys' interests') is a real one. Rather, the possibility is that the curriculum is already subtly infused with hegemonic male values, for example in the way history is represented. The need to promote girls' participation in subjects such as maths and technology is ever present, as evidenced by the shortage of females going into science/technology based employment. Bilton *et al* (1996) found that the illustrations in science textbooks portrayed four males for every one female. Most important of all, however, is the principle of a broad and balanced curriculum that aims to develop breadth and balance in pupils. Belief in such a principle commits us to opposing narrowing boys' outlook because of our expectations that males are interested only in football.

The key word here is *expectation*. The effects of teacher expectations on pupil performance are well known and suitably summarised in texts such as Alexander (2000, 358), Muijs and Reynolds (2001a, 63-65) and Long (2000, 126-128). The research summarised in these texts confirms that teacher expectations based upon their judgements of pupils do significantly affect teacher behaviour towards pupils and consequent pupil attainment. A self-fulfilling prophecy still prevails. Teachers' cultural expectations may be even more significant. Evidence for this can be found in the continuing way in which African-Caribbean boys are judged to be less academically able and more confrontational in their attitudes to teachers. Gillborn (1990) and Mac an Ghaill (1988) have convincingly demonstrated the effects of teachers' cultural expectations in this context. When the cultural expectations and prejudices of politicians and tabloid journalists are added, the cocktail becomes lethal indeed.

Alexander (1984) developed a comprehensive argument that children's potential and performance were dependent upon teachers' subject knowledge and teachers' knowledge of the children. We take up this argument because of the evidence that the majority of primary school teachers lack subject knowledge or skill in music and football, through no fault of their own. An extremely subtle disempowerment of women teachers occurs when boys realise during PE lessons that they know more about football than their teacher does. We have observed PE lessons where teachers seem quite oblivious to the fact that certain boys have far higher skill levels attained outside school than are supposedly being developed in the lesson. Ashley's study of boy singers reveals that the same thing is happening in music. Boys who sang in a well known church choir were seen to be far more proficient in music than their primary school teachers (Ashley, 2002a).

This issue has nothing to do with teacher gender but everything to do with teaching competence. It was an unfortunate action by the Teacher Training Agency to promote boy stereotypes through its '*Every Good Boy Deserves Football*' campaign (TTA advert, 1999). It is too early to evaluate whether the TTA campaign to recruit more men was effective, although at the time of writing there are slight indications that the fall in recruitment has been reversed. But at what cost? The advert implies that female teachers are incompetent in football. It is important to distinguish rhetoric from reality. For example a scheme promoted at the time of writing by Arsenal football club crassly claims that it is 'trying to break the trend for girls to take the literacy course while boys opt for football' whilst in practice sending six young men, including one who 'worships Arsenal', to work in a primary school (Klein, 2002) To preserve the core argument of this book, teacher gender must be disentangled from other factors that might affect boys' attitudes to schooling.

Although our research suggests that in relation to the core curriculum boys are not concerned about the gender of their teacher, they do notice gendered behaviour of teachers with regard to sport. For example, Colin in Y4. answered our question: '*What about football?* (Colin smiles) *Do lady teachers do enough sport?*' thus: '*Mr Jameson does football, but there should be more females. They'd be as good as the males. There are not enough girls playing football.*' MA: '*Would you play with girls?*' Colin: '*Yeah ... but not <u>all</u> girls!*' This seems a reasonable position for an eight year old boy to take, and worth encouraging. In contrast Dean, a Y6 boy interviewed at home, had this to say about SAT results which appeared to suggest boys' underperformance. Dean: '*Girls have got bigger brains so that they can remember where they left their handbag.*' MA: '*Is that sexist Dean?*' Dean: '*Yeah.*' MA: '*So where do you get that idea from?*' Dean: '*My football coach*' (Dean is referring here to a football club, not a school).

Kate, however, had a story to tell at interview. She is a primary teacher who is well qualified to coach football, recommended to us for interview by a university PE colleague. When we asked her about the coaching of the school football team, we discovered that she had been 'relegated' to training the younger children, while some Dads had taken over the 'proper' team. This is a not unfamilar situation. Primary schools which rely on Dads to coach their football team, are sending a strong message. There is no reason to suppose that the Dads are necessarily competent coaches or suitable role models. A well known club mini-side was suspended from a rugby tournament because of the poor behaviour of Dads on the touch line. We have evidence from our present study, however, that some female primary teachers are complicit in this perpetuation of male hegemony.

The comments of Colin's class teacher, Sandra, are revealing. MA: '*An issue is that some women don't do much sport, but this does seem to be important to boys.*' Sandra: '*I'd kill them if they said I don't like sport, out there in my track suit. Perhaps I don't look the part, with my scarf and wooly hat!* (changes mood) *I thought it was totally wrong that Mark did Jennie and Rachel's PE because he thought they wouldn't do it. Jennie used to be a secondary PE teacher!*' A number of things seem to be going on here. Sandra seems to regard it as important that she should be seen to teach sport and has strong feelings about teachers' roles and examples. Mark appears to take the stereotypical male view that the women wouldn't do the sport properly, whilst Jennie, an ex secondary school PE teacher is possibly better qualified to do it than he. Remarkably though, she is content for him to promote this attitude and set this example. Young Colin seems to be fair and open minded, but is being set a poor example. In Dean's case, we see how easy it is for male coaches in football clubs to change the open minded attitude shown by Colin.

Harriet, a mature female teacher we interviewed in another school, seems content to collude with the attitude typified by Mark. MA: '*So what do men teachers do?*' Harriet '*They're going to run football with vigour, they're going to do Mrs Anderson's PE lessons for her, maybe going to be greatly loved father figures, or enthusiastically hero worshipped for running football and getting boys enthusiastic about sport. I'm already planning swaps for next year so they'll do my PE.*' The temptation to adopt a judgmental attitude, praising Colin and Sandra, and condemning Harriet and Mark should be resisted. The issues are complicated. It is easy to regard the issue as a simple gender problem. However, we believe it to be more a problem of school and curriculum management, and ultimately democracy in social organisation.

If football has come to be stereotyped as a 'boy thing' and has the unfortunate status of a monoculture for boys, then it is probably equally true that singing has become stereotyped as 'girlie' and music regarded as a feminine subject. Roulston and Mills (2000), for example, are amongst those to have implied that music is a feminised area of schooling. Sources such as Hanley (1998) or Ross (1995) paint a picture of music education as a low status area dominated by women. Green (1997) uses words such as 'cissy' and 'un-macho' in an account of boys' non-participation in school music and singing. And this is not a recent phenomenon. Koza (1992) examined accounts of boys' non-participation in music between 1914 and 1924, and his work shows that this is not a new aspect of the problem-with-boys. More likely boys' participation in music as opposed to sport has always required a dedicated input from those who consider it important to broaden cultural horizons.

Boys' non-participation in singing is not a simple issue of gender nor role modelling. For the majority of primary school children, it is probable that their earliest encounters with singing are at school assemblies or Christmas carol services. Behind this simple fact lie considerable complexities, of which gender is but one. The idea of singing as 'girlie' is perverse, because famous boys' choirs such as King's College Cambridge have dominated the cultural scene for centuries. Issues such as social class may be at least as significant as gender because boys who sing in cathedral choirs are for the most part educated in fee paying schools.

However, one of the studies that have contributed to this book was of the choir of a major city church, in which the boys were drawn from local primary and comprehensive schools (Ashley, 2002a). This study revealed certain key similarities between football and singing. The boys achieved much more in music outside their schools than in them, and were forthright in their condemnation of school music. The following extracts are typical. 'Our school choir is rubbish, boring, absolute rubbish' (Y5 boy). '*Our school choir is embarrassing, they sing silly little songs like Red, Red Robin*' (Y6 boy). '*The quality of the singing is terrible and they only have words. No music. They just teach us the melody and we don't sing in parts. The irony is that the boys who want to be in the choir can read music. They just sing tacky musicals. I prefer proper choral singing'* (Y7 boy). Particularly strong confirmation of the 'sing like a girl' issue comes from this Y6 boy describing his experience at school: *'I'm teased and called a girl because I had a high singing part in Oliver. They think only girls can sing that high. They need education.'*

A significant feature of this choir is that it is an all male environment, boys and men, with a male director. As reported elsewhere (Ashley, 2003), hegemonic masculinity was a feature. Role models provided by the choir men included boasts of beer drinking exploits and frequent discussion of football results. The 'sing like a girl' insult was used by the choirmaster to disapprove of singing he considered feeble in tone. A fourteen year old in a group interview told us *'You must understand that boys find girls en masse intimidating'* when he recalled experiences of primary school. The intimidating effect on a seven or eight year old boy confronted by a mass of girls was the reason given by the group for the dominance of girls in school choirs. It does tend to suggest that boys' self-worth protection and inner confidence may be vulnerable in the face of secretly perceived but unacknowledged female power.

This research is still ongoing. We have sought out primary schools where boys sing enthusiastically and join the choir and have found some. In one school, the boys had actually asked to have a choir of their own and the female music teacher was pleased to oblige them. Alice, the music teacher at another school, was alarmed at the prospect that her boys might be put off by any suggestion it was 'girlie' to sing. Boys sang loudly and enthusiastically at her hymn practice. Alice was herself a skilled musician who exuded enthusiasm. The female teacher at the third school was also musically skilled. The idea emerging here, which we need to test further, is that it does not necessarily take a man to make boys sing, but rather a musically competent teacher of either gender.

Where should we go?

The teacher we named Maureen was critical of the nature of the National Curriculum and the National Literacy Strategy. She gave the example of a dance week as an important contribution to the children's educational and cultural development but noted sadly how difficult it was to '*fit it in*'. What she and Dee were clear about was that a curriculum is required that matches the pupils' needs and takes into account the richness of their cultural lives. Such a curriculum is delivered by good teachers not gendered teachers; a point not lost on our child informants who couldn't choose between a male or female teacher '*because I don't know how they teach*'. So reasons given for the gap in the performance of boys and girls in standard assessments are simplistic. And so are the ideas advanced to change the position. The contention that there are some subjects or activities that are natural for boys brings with it the corollary that there are subjects that are natural for girls. Anyone offering this suggestion would be quickly reminded of the recent and past history of feminist theory and action in no uncertain terms.

It may be that the 'boys crisis' will lead to a careful and objective review of the primary curriculum and pedagogy. Ideally rationality rather than knee jerk response should determine educational policy. In which case the traditional subjects of mathematics, science and language study would still be on the curriculum, but recognised as significant cultural products, not access skills to some later examination or employment. Take the case of mathematics, the subject most often proposed as 'natural' for boys. Currently it is presented as utilitarian – the sort of knowledge that is essential for progression to a good career. What is needed is a rich and balanced curriculum that rejects this utilitarian and masculised view of mathematics and presents it as an exciting and significant cultural activity, one that can be found in every culture. This means more than using Islamic patterns as examples or telling children that the concept of zero entered European thinking from India via Arab culture. It means demonstrating the fascination, enjoyment and relevance of mathematics to children's interests.

Maureen stressed the importance of an *'interesting, culturally and linguistically relevant and enjoyable curriculum.'* The change that is needed concerns not the gender of the teacher but how their pupils learn mathematics, and how they understand why mathematics is to be taught. What might be needed at Key Stage 2 could be more enthusiastic 'specialists' alongside the class teacher. Similar arguments can be made for science and language studies. The expressive curriculum is, however, crucial. Diplomas in Expressive Arts/Studies are available to students over the age of sixteen, usually in Further Education colleges, but strangely there are few opportunities at Key Stage 1 and 2. We have shown that boys can and do enjoy music including singing and dance. There is a rich popular culture in dance forms. Dance competitions were a a popular feature of 'blues/sound system' venues in the 1970s, 80s and 90s, 'skanking' among African-Caribbean males. Yet there is little evidence that dance and music are important and valued parts of the curriculum. Breadth, balance, richness and relevance require more teaching of the expressive arts, not less. To assume that dance is a female interest is to ignore both the history of dance and its contemporary role in British culture.

The generalist teacher is usually as ill equipped to teach dance and music as to teach PE and sport. There is here a fundamental issue of democracy and equality of opportunity. If self-determination is a democratic right, then boys are denied this right by two features of primary school life. The first, which is equally applicable to girls, is the lack of teacher expertise in the expressive subjects. Teachers with the relevant teaching subject expertise are more likely to work in fee paying than maintained schools. The second feature, which applies more specifically to boys, is the failure to counter the boy stereotype of football monoculture. It is through this failure that boys are genuinely disadvantaged over girls. Far more is done to facilitate the raising of aspirations for girls to succeed in mathematics, technology and physical science than for boys to succeed in music, art, dance and drama.

Reform of the curriculum will require new training and new partnerships. Dance may be best taught by expert performer teachers, as in Further and Higher Education. For music to be properly taught in school, musicians are needed. Involving experts is not just a matter of 'swapping for PE'. It is about recognising that there are experts, and that their number can be increased through appropriate training. The issue is the promotion of expertise, not of gender. Most expert and enthusiastic workers in the expressive arts might not wish to devote themselves entirely to primary teaching, in which case new ways of working will be forged. This is not as difficult as it seems. Theatre in Education is an illustration of what is possible.

There remains the question of role models and mentoring. Our data shows clearly that all children need good role models and that in primary schools the teacher is the 'significant other'. The boys we interviewed told us that it was not the gender of the teacher that mattered but their qualities as a teacher. They want teachers who teach well, teachers they can respect and who respect them. Teachers need to be caring but they are not expected to be substitute mothers. They are expected to keep good order, to create an environment in which learning can go on. As one boy put it '*I'd like a man teacher who could solve problems and that just like Mrs. B does.*' Primary aged pupils have always been taught mainly by women.

Involving people from outside the school as role models and mentors has been urged on schools by policy makers and commentators. The idea that bringing a successful male into school to enthuse the boys, to change them from rejectors of learning to enthusiastic scholars, over-simplifies important issues. No matter how male he might be, the life of the middle class professional and the attitudes and values that go with it are as remote from working class pupils as the lives of their female teachers. Maureen's school (Chapter 8), offered an approach to role modelling in which (female) teachers approached the issue with sophistication that is well ahead of the pronouncements of policy makers. What is important is enabling the pupils to identify themselves as significant people in their communities and, when they are older, the wider world. This means the celebration not of conventional success – 'Here is a x kind of lawyer' – but bringing adults from all walks of life into school to talk about their jobs and their roles in families and communities.

Children need to see that success is not simply about a BMW and a wallet full of money but about having respect for the job you do and the role you can play. If we genuinely want a fair and inclusive society, we need to model a society in which people are valued for who they are and the way they relate to others. We need to be wary of society models that show a male head teacher ruling a school of females, and equally wary of society models that promote male success only in terms of financial reward.

Finally, while we acknowledge that there is differential achievement and that currently girls do better than boys in national tests and examinations, we challenge the way this has been attributed to a problem with women and girls. We fear that lurking behind some of the commentaries is a rejection of the slight advances that women and girls have made, for instance, claims that the move towards course work rather than closed book exams advantages girls because boys like to get things over and done with. Maybe some boys do not see the necessity to work diligently in schools because all around them they see success defined as positions of power and influence, still dominated by men. Schools, whatever the gender of their staff, are part of a masculised discourse that is expressed in how they are organised and made accountable. The hard driven target agenda set externally, and the way Ofsted inspects and judges schools, provide further evidence of this discourse. Why bother to work if you can see that the glittering prizes are the result not of scholarship but of gender privilege?

Bibliography

Ainsworth, M. (1967) *Infancy in Uganda: Infant Care and the Growth of Attachment*, Baltimore: John Hopkins University Press

Ainsworth, M. and Wittig, B. (1969) Attachment and Exploratory Behaviour of One Year Olds in a Strange Situation, In B. Foss (ed.) *Determinants of Infant Behaviour* IV. London: Methuen

Albisetti, J. (1993) The Feminisation of teaching in the nineteenth century: a comparative perspective, *History of Education*, 22 (3) 253-263

Alexander, R. (1984) *Primary Teaching*, London: Holt, Rinehart and Winston

Alexander, R. (2000) *Culture and Pedagogy.* Oxford: Blackwell

Ashley, M. (1992) The Validity of Sociometric Status, *Educational Research.* 34 (2) 149-154

Ashley, M. (1993) Peer Attachments and Social Deviancy in the Primary School. Unpublished MPhil thesis, University of the West of England, Bristol

Ashley, M. (2001) Caring for the Boys: lessons from attachment theory. Paper presented at the *British Education Research Association* meeting. Leeds, 13th-15th September

Ashley, M. (2002a) Singing, Gender and Health: perspectives from boys singing in a church choir. *Health Education.* 102 (4) 180-187

Ashley, M. (2002b) The Spiritual, the Cultural and the Religious: what can we learn from a study of boy choristers? *International Journal of Children's Spirituality.* 7 (3) 257-272

Ashley, M. (2003) 'You Must Understand That We Find Girls en Masse Intimidating': Maximum masculinities as boys perform a girlie activity. *Revisiting Feminist Perspectives on Gender and Education.* Gender and Education Association, 4th International Conference, University of Sheffield, 14th-16th April

Askew, S. and Ross, C. (1988) *Boys don't cry: boys and sexism in education.* Buckingham: Open University Press

Atkinson, A. and Wilson, D. (2003) The Widening Gender Gap in English Schools CMPO *Market and Public Organisation* 8: January 4-7 University of Bristol

Balchin, T. (2002) Male Teachers in Primary Education, *Forum* 44 (1) 29-33

Barrett, M. and Trevitt, J. (1991) *Attachment Behaviour and the Schoolchild,* London: Routledge

Biddulph, S. (1997) *Raising Boys*, London: Harper Collins/Thorsons

Bilton, T., Bonnett, K., Joines, P., Skinner, D., Stanworth, M. and Webster, A. (1996) *Introductory Sociology* (3rd edn.) London: MacMillan

Blunkett, D. (2000) Boys must improve at the same rate as girls, DfES press release 20th August

Blurton-Jones, N. (1974) Ethology and Early Socialisation. in M. Richards (ed.) *The Integration of a Child into a Social World*, Cambridge: Cambridge University Press

Board of Education (1905) *Handbook of suggestions for elementary school teachers.* London: HMSO

Board of Education (1931) *Report of the Consultative Committee on the Primary School*, London: HMSO

Board of Education (1933) *Report of the Consultative Committee on Infant and Nursery Schools*, London: HMSO

Bowlby, J. (1952) *Maternal Care and Mental Health*, Geneva: World Health Organisation

Bowlby, J. (1969) *Attachment and Loss. Vol. 1: Attachment*, London: Hogarth Press

Bricheno, P. and Thornton, M. (2002) Staff Gender Balance in Primary Schools. Paper presented at BERA Annual Meeting, Exeter 12th-14th September

Brophy, J. and Evertson, C. (1976) *Learning from Teaching: a developmental perspective*, Boston: Allyn and Bacon

Byers, S. (1998) Co-ordinated Action to Tackle Boys' Underachievement. Speech presented to the Eleventh International Congress for School Effectiveness and Improvement, UMIST, 5th January

CACE (1967) Children and the Primary Schools, *The Plowden Report*. London: HMSO

Carrington B (2002) A Quintessentially Feminine Domain? Student teachers' construction of primary teaching as a career, *Educational Studies* 28 (3) 287-303

Carrington, B. and Skelton, C. (forthcoming) Re-Thinking 'Role Models': Equal Opportunities in teacher recruitment in England and Wales. *Journal of Education Policy*

Channel 4 Television. (2002) Boys Alone. *Cutting Edge* documentary

Clarke, K. (1985). Public and private children: infant education in the 1820s and 1830s. in C. Steedman, C. Urwin and V. Waldkerdine (eds.) *Language, Gender and Childhood*, London: Routledge

Clift, S. and Hancox G. (2001) The benefits of singing: findings from preliminary surveys with a university college choral society, *Journal of the Royal Society for the Promotion of Health*, 121 (4) 248-256

Coard, B. (1971) *How the West Indian Child Is Made Educationally Subnormal in the British School System*, London: New Beacon Books

Cohen S. (1987) *Folk Devils and Moral Panics: the creation of Mods and Rockers*, Blackwell: Oxford

Connell, R. (1995) *Masculinities*. Cambridge: Polity Press

Connolly, P. (1998) *Racism, Gender, Identities and Young Children*, London: Routledge

Covington, M. (2000) Goal theory, motivation and school achievement: An integrative review, *Annual Review of Psychology*, 51 171-200

Creemers, B. and Reezigt, G. (1996) School level conditions affecting the effectiveness of instruction. *School Effectiveness and School Improvement*, 7 197-228

Crook, D. (1997). Challenge, Response and Dilution: a revisionist view of the Emergency Training Scheme for Teachers, 1945-1951. *Cambridge Journal of Education*, 27 (3) 379-390

DES (1965) *Demand for the Supply of Teachers 1963-1986. 9th Report of the National Advisory Council of the Training and Supply of Teachers*, London: HMSO

DES (1978) *Primary Education in England. A survey by HM Inspectors of Schools*, London: HMSO

DES (1982) *Education 5-9: an illustrative survey of 80 first schools in England*, London: HMSO

DfES (2002) NPQH Consultation Document DfES, 15th March

Dent, H. (1977) *The Training of Teachers in England and Wales 1800-1975*, London: Hodder and Stoughton

Duffy, M. (2002) Achievement Gap *Times Educational Supplement* 15 Nov 16

Evans, W. (1992) Gender Stereotyping and the Training of Female Elementary Teachers: the experience of Victorian Wales, *History of Education*, 21.

Foster, T. and Newman, E. (2001) Men Mentoring and Masculinity: The Role of Mentoring in the Recruitment of Young Men into Primary Teaching. Paper presented to the *Teacher Supply and Retention Conference*. University of North London, June 12th

Foster, V. Kimmel, M. and Skelton, C. (2001) What about the boys? An overview of the debates. In W. Martino and B. Meyenn (eds.) *What About the Boys? Issues of masculinity in schools*. Buckingham: Open University Press

Francis, B. (1999) Lads, Lasses and (New) Labour: 14-16-year-old students' responses to the 'laddish behaviour and boys' underachievement debate, *British Journal of Sociology of Education*. 20 (3) 355-370

Francis, B. (2000) *Boys, Girls and Achievement*. London: Routledge/ Falmer

Freke, M. (2001) What is Worse Than a Reluctant Organist? – No Organist at All. *Church Times*. 10 Nov

Galley M. (2000) Male Preschool Teachers Face Skepticism But Earn Acceptance, *Education Week* 26 Jan

Gilbert, R and Gilbert, P. (1998) *Masculinity Goes to School*, London: Routledge

Gillborn, D. (1990) *'Race', Ethnicity and Education: Teaching and Learning in Multi-Ethnic Schools*, London: Unwin Hyman/Routledge

Gipps, C. and Murphy, P. (1998) Boys' failure is everyone's problem, *Times Educational Supplement* 30th January

Gorrard, S. (2000) *Education and social justice : the changing composition of schools and its implications*, Cardiff: University of Wales Press

Green, L. (1997) *Music, Gender, Education*. Cambridge: Cambridge University Press

Grosvenor, I. and Lawn, M. (2001) This is what we are and this is what we do: teacher identity and teacher work in Twentieth Century England, *Pedagogy, Culture and Society* 9 (3) 355-370

Hanley, B. (1998) Gender in Secondary Music Education in British Columbia. *British Journal of Music Education*. 15 (1) 51-69

Harlow, H. and Harlow, M. (1971) Psychopathology in Monkeys. In H. Kimmel (ed.) *Experimental Pyschopathology*. New York: Academic Press

Haughton E (2002) Hitting the Right Button, *Education Guardian* 19 Nov, 2-3

Haywood, C. and Mac an Ghaill, M. (1996) Schooling Masculinities. In M. Mac an Ghaill (ed.) *Understanding Masculinities: Social Relations and Cultural Arenas*. Buckingham: Open University Press

Heard, D. (1978) From Object Relations Theory to Attachment Theory: a basis for family therapy. *British Journal of Medical Psychology*, 51 67-76

Hebdige, D. (1979) *Subculture: the meaning of style*, London: Routledge

Heinig, R. (1976) A descriptive study of teacher-pupil tactile communication in grades 4 through 6, *Dissertation Abstracts International*, 36/12A, 7948.

Hickey, C and Fitzclarence, L. (2000) Regimes of Risk: Young Males' Perceptions of Disruptive and Antisocial Behaviour in the Context of Schooling. Paper presented to *British Educational Research Association Annual Conference*, Cardiff, 7-9 Sept

Howard, D. and Szymanski, J. (2000) Listener Perception of Girls and Boys in an English Cathedral Choir. ICMPC proceedings paper

Howard, D., Barlow, C. and Welch, G. (2000) *Vocal Production and Listener Perception of Trained Girls and Boys in the English Cathedral Choir.* Paper presented at International Society for Music Education, 18th International seminar, University of Utah, Salt Lake City July 8-14

Humphries, S. (1981) Hooligans or Rebels? *An oral history of working class childhood and youth 1889-1939*, Oxford: Blackwell

Jackson, C. (2002a) Laddishness as a Self-worth Protection Strategy. *Gender and Education* 14 (1) 37-51

Jackson, C. (2002b) Can Single-sex Classes in Co-educational Schools Enhance the Learning Experiences of Girls and/or Boys? An exploration of pupils' perceptions. *British Educational Research Journal* 28 (1) 37-48

King, J. (1998) *Uncommon Caring: learning from men who teach young children*, New York: Teachers College Press

Klein, R. (2002) 'The A Team'. *Times Educational Supplement*, 'Friday' 8 Nov, 10-13

Koza, J. (1992) The Missing Males and Other Gender Related Issues in Music Education, 1914-1924. *Journal of Research in Music Education.* 41 (3) 212-232

Lawn, M. (1987) *Servants of the state : the contested control of teaching 1900-1930*, Brighton: Falmer

Lewis, P. and Weston, C. (2002) Creating Boyzones. Paper presented to BERA annual conference, University of Exeter, 12-14 Sept

Long, M. (2000) *The Psychology of Education.* London: Falmer

Lorenz, K. (1937) The Establishment of the Instinct Concept. In *Studies in Animal and Human Behaviour*, Vol. 1. (trans. R. Martin.) London: Methuen

Lovegrove, E. (2002) Adolescents, Appearance and Anti-Bullying Strategies. Unpublished PhD Thesis, University of the West of England, Bristol

Mac an Ghaill, M. (1988) *Young, Gifted and Black: student-teacher relations in the schooling of black youth*, Buckingham: Open University Press

Mac an Ghaill, M. (1994) *The Making of Men: Masculinities, Sexualities and Schooling.* Buckingham: Open University Press

Mac an Ghaill, M. (ed.) (1996) *Understanding Masculinities.* Buckingham: Open University Press

Mac an Ghaill, M. (2002) Beyond Role Models: Conceptual and Methodological Issues. Keynote address at *Society Modeling and Inclusion, Recovering the Agenda from the Media.* Centre for Research in Education and Democracy, University of the West of England, Bristol, 17th October

Mead G. H. (1962) *Mind, self, and society: from the standpoint of a social behaviorist*, Chicago I: University of Chicago Press

Millett, A. (1999) Teaching Tomorrow – Challenges and Opportunities, TTA 8

Milner, D. (1983) *Children and Race: Ten Years On*, London: Ward Lock Educational

Ministry of Education (1945) A guide to the educational system of England and Wales. *Ministry of Education Pamphlet* no 2. London: HMSO

Ministry of Education (1951) *Training and Supply of Teachers. First Report of the National Advisory Council July 1949 to February 1951,* London: HMSO

Ministry of Education (1959) *Primary Education. Suggestions for the consideration of teachers and others concerned with the work of Primary Schools,* London: HMSO

Muijs, D. and Reynolds, D. (2001a) *Effective Teaching: evidence and practice,* London: Paul Chapman

Muijs, D. and Reynolds, D. (2001b) The effective teaching of mathematics – a review of research, *School Leadership and Management* 11 (3) 273-303

Neill, S. St J. (1991) Children's Responses to Touch – a questionnaire study. *British Educational Research Journal.* 17 (2) 149-163

Noble, C. and Bradford, W. (2000) *Getting it Right: for boys ... and girls.* London: Routledge

Philips, A. (1993) *The Trouble with Boys: parenting the men of the future.* London: Harper Collins/Pandora

Pollard, A. (1985) *The Social World of the Primary School.* London: Holt, Reinhart and Winston

Pratt, S. (2000) Wanna be my friend: A study of male primary school friendship, *Primary Teaching Studies* 11 (2) 43-52

Pratt, S. and Burn, E. (2000) Every Good Boy Deserves Football. Paper presented to *British Educational Research Association annual conference,* Cardiff, 7-9 Sept

Reay, D. (2001) The paradox of contemporary feminities, in B. Francis and C. Skelton (eds.) *Investigating Gender; Contemporary perspectives in education.* Buckingham: Open University Press

Reay, D. (2002) Shaun's Story: troubling discourses of white working-class masculinities, *Gender and Education* 14 (3) 221-234

Rendall, J. (1990) *Women in an Industrializing Society: England 1750-1880.* Oxford: Blackwell

Renold, E. (2000) Presumed Innocence: Sexualised bullying and harassment in the primary school, Paper presented to *5th Conference of the European Sociological Association,* Helsinki, August 28th-September 1st.

Renold, E. (2001) 'Tales of the Unexpected': researching sexuality in the primary school. In L. Pugsley and T. Welland (eds.) *Ethical Dilemmas in Qualitative Research.* Aldershot: Ashgate

Robinson, K. [Chairman] (1999) All Our Futures: Creativity, Culture and Education. *Report of the National Advisory Committeee on Creative and Cultural Education.* Sudbury: DfEE

Ross, M. (1995) What's Wrong with School Music? *British Journal of Music Education.* 12 (3) 185-201

Roulston, K. and Mills, M. (2000) Male Teachers in Feminised Areas: Marching to the Beat of the Men's Movement Drums? *Oxford Review of Education,* 26 (2) 221-237

Sainsbury, J. and Jackson, D. (1996) *Challenging Macho Values: practical ways of working with adolescent boys.* London: Falmer

Sale, G. (2002) Master's thesis, Hull University. Quoted in the *Times Educational Supplement,* November 29th 3

Silver, H. (1994) *Good Schools Effective Schools.* London: Cassell

Skelton, C. (2001) *Schooling the Boys: masculinities and primary schooling.* Buckingham: Open University Press

Skelton, C. (2002a) Keynote address at *Society Modeling and Inclusion, Recovering the Agenda from the Media.* Centre for Research in Education and Democracy, University of the West of England, Bristol, 17 Oct

Skelton, C. (2002b) The 'Feminisation of Schooling' or 'Re-masculinising' Primary Education. *International Studies in Sociology of Education* 12 (1)

Slukin, A. (1981) *Growing Up in the Playground: the social development of children.* London: Routledge and Kegan Paul

Smithers, R. (2002) Teacher colleges recruit fewer men, *The Guardian* 15 July

Standing Committee on Education and Training of the Australian parliament House of Representatives (2002) http://www.dest.gov.au/edu/gen_ ed_pubs.htm

Stone, M. (1981) *The Education of the Black Child in Britain: the myth of multiracial education,* London: Fontana

Thornton, K. (2002) Heads don't need that vision thing. *Times Educational Supplement,* 29 Nov, 3

Times Educational Supplement (2002) Leading article 13 Sept 22

TTA (2002) symposium 'Men Teaching In Primary and Early Years'. 15 July

Vogt, F. (2002) A Caring Teacher: explorations into primary school teachers' professional identity and ethic of care. *Gender and Education* 14 (3) 251-264.

Walkerdine, V. (1981) Sex, power and pedagogy, *Screen Education,* 38 14-24

Wardle, D. (1977) *English popular education 1780-1975,* Cambridge: Cambridge University Press

Warrington, M. and Younger, M. (2000) The Other Side of the Gender Gap. *Gender and Education,* 12 (4) 493-508

Wheldall, K., Bevan, K. and Shortall, K (1986) A Touch of Reinforcement: the effects of contingent teacher touch on the classroom behaviour of young children. *Educational Review* 38 (3) 207-216

Wilby, P. (1998) Fashions change but both boys and girls need attention; Opinion *Times Educational Supplement* 16 Jan

Willis, P. (1977) *Learning to Labour: how working class kids get working class jobs,* London: Saxon House

Wilson, G. (accessed02/12/02) http://www.canteach.gov.uk/publications/community/research/grant/97-98/tta99_17.pdf

Winnicott, D. (1965) *The Maturational Process and the Facilitating Environment,* London: Hogarth Press

Woods, P. (1976) Having a laugh: an antidote to schooling, in M. Hammersly and P. Woods (eds.) *The Process of Schooling: a sociological reader,* London: Routledge and Kegan Paul

Index